ANNABEL WRIGLEY

My Sew
WORKSHOP

Simple Guide to Skills & Supplies

40 Fun Projects to Stitch & Share

FunStitch
STUDIO
an imprint of C&T Publishing

Text copyright © 2022 by Annabel Wrigley

Photography and artwork copyright © 2022 by C&T Publishing, Inc.

Publisher: Amy Barrett-Daffin

Creative Director: Gailen Runge

Editors: Liz Aneloski, Cynthia Bix, and Lee Jonsson

Associate Editor: Jennifer Warren

Technical Editors: Carolyn Aune, Gailen Runge, Amanda Siegfried, Teresa Stroin, and Nanette S. Zeller

Cover/Book Designer: April Mostek

Production Coordinator: Tim Manibusan

Illustrators: Jessica Jenkins, Tim Manibusan, and Kirstie L. Pettersen

Photography Assistant: Gabriel Martinez

Front cover photography by Kristen Gardner

Photography by Kristen Gardner, unless otherwise noted

Published by FunStitch Studio, an imprint of C&T Publishing, Inc., P.O. Box 1456, Lafayette, CA 94549

Library of Congress Cataloging-in-Publication Data

Names: Wrigley, Annabel, 1972- author.

Title: My sewing workshop : simple guide to skills & supplies : 40 fun projects to stitch & share / Annabel Wrigley.

Description: Lafayette, CA : FunStitch Studio, an imprint of C&T Publishing, Inc., [2022] | Audience: Ages 8-14.

Identifiers: LCCN 2021062601 | ISBN 9781644032688 (trade paperback) | ISBN 9781644032695 (ebook)

Subjects: LCSH: Sewing--Juvenile literature. | Textile crafts--Juvenile literature.

Classification: LCC TT712 .W748 2022 | DDC 646/.1--dc23/eng/20220131

LC record available at https://lccn.loc.gov/2021062601

Printed in China

10 9 8 7 6 5 4 3 2 1

Contents

91

CASES, POUCHES, AND MORE

74

CELEBRATIONS

113

101

ORGANIZATION

BEDROOM

PETS

216

220

209

How to Use This Book

In this book, some of the projects are pretty easy, and some are a bit more challenging. You'll notice that each project has a symbol at the top. Here's what each symbol means.

● **EASY PEASY**

Start with these projects, especially if you are not super comfy yet with using your sewing machine. These are fun hand-sewing and craft projects that you'll have no trouble finishing.

●● **A TEENY BIT MORE CHALLENGING**

You'll need a little confidence for these projects. You should be comfortable with using the sewing machine and hand sewing. You are going to have so much fun with these!

●●● **TAKE YOUR TIME AND ASK FOR HELP**

These projects need some patience and a great attitude. If you really know your way around your sewing machine, go for it! I know you can do it. You may want to ask for help from an adult or other experienced sewist. We all need a little help sometimes!

☆TIP

Practicing your skills on the easier projects in the book will help you gain confidence to tackle the more challenging ones!

The Rules of Sewing

I think it is so important for you to go into your sewing experience with a good knowledge of some do's and don'ts. I sure don't want to be telling you what to do, but there are some good things to know if you want to have a fun and successful sewing experience.

Keeping It Calm, Cool, and Collected

Yes, sewing is pretty fun and relaxing, but sometimes you may feel pressure to finish a project really fast or to speed up because you think it is important to always finish first. You may even feel pressure to sew better than someone else. You know what? In my classes, there is no pressure to be anything other than yourself. Be an individual, learn at your own pace, create your OWN work, and take pride in your individuality!

Express Yourself

Who says you can't put orange and purple together or mix a plaid with a polka dot? This is your project, and it is up to you to decide how wild and crazy or simple and sedate your project will be. Think about the person who will receive the gift and his or her personality and then go for it.

Slow Down!

It is amazing to me how many kids just want to finish a project as fast as possible. I think it is so important for you to start each new project with a deep breath and a whole lot of patience. You will love your work so much more if you just take the time to slow down—I promise!

Practice, Practice, Practice

You have to practice when you play soccer, do gymnastics, or even play the piano. It is the same with sewing. You can't expect to be able to sew a complicated project if you haven't practiced those sewing skills.

My best advice is to start with this easy practice exercise.

1. Start with a plain piece of fabric and use a ruler and an erasable pen to draw some straight lines on the fabric.

2. Thread your sewing machine with a bright-colored thread. Refer to your sewing machine manual if you need to.

3. Starting at the tippy top of the line, sew all the way to the bottom, working hard to keep your sewing on top of the line. You may start out a little wonky, but I pinky swear that after a few times you will feel more and more confident.

4. After you have mastered this, turn over the fabric and line up the edge of the presser foot with the stitch line you made before and sew, keeping the presser foot right on the line. Go ahead and practice this on all the lines.

Now that you are feeling super confident, try drawing a big zigzag pattern on top of the fabric. Change your thread color and work on sewing the straight section and then pivoting at the zig (or is that the zag?).

↑ **1** Stop at the turn.

↑ **2** Turn the handwheel so that the needle is down.

↑ **3** Lift the presser foot.

↑ **4** Turn the fabric.

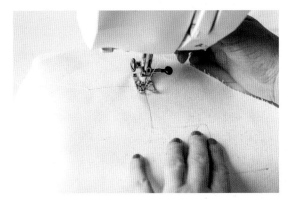

↑ **5** Drop the presser foot and off you go!

Don't stop there! Try drawing some curves and other crazy patterns. At the end of this exercise, just iron to erase the pen marks, and your fabric will look awesomely colorful and creative and will be begging to be used in a project (a bag could be cute!).

That was easy!

What Will I Need?

Each project has a whole list of supplies that are important for that particular project. There are a few things most of them have in common, and those are the basic supplies you will need!

Basic Supplies

SEWING MACHINE

Of course, you will need a sewing machine for the majority of projects in this book, but do you know how to use one? Take the time to dig out the manual that came with your machine. If it has mysteriously disappeared, jump on the Internet. You will be amazed by how much valuable information you can find about your sewing machine!

SEWING MACHINE NEEDLES

Ever been to the store and been totally confused by the wall of sewing machine needles? Lucky for you that all our sewing machine projects only require the use of universal needles. Yay! Needle size 80/12 or 100/14 will work great for the fabrics we are sewing.

PINS

These are important to hold your work together for sewing. Straight pearl-head pins and flat plastic flower-head pins are my favorites. The longer length is perfect for our projects.

RULER

I always have a ton of clear quilting rulers hanging about! My most useful one is my clear 6½˝ × 24˝ quilter's ruler.

SCISSORS

A good sharp pair of scissors is super important, as I don't recommend the use of rotary cutters for kids. Make sure to have two pairs of scissors, one for fabric and one for paper. Paper cutting can really dull those fabric scissors!

SEAM RIPPER

A seam ripper is a new sewist's best friend. Always have one handy. This tool will help you rip out those "oops" stitches easily and quickly. The sharp tip helps you cut stitching without putting a huge hole in your fabric.

HAND SEWING NEEDLES

Quite a few projects in this book require some hand sewing skills. Make sure you have some good sharp needles on hand. You will need some with bigger eyes when you sew with embroidery floss.

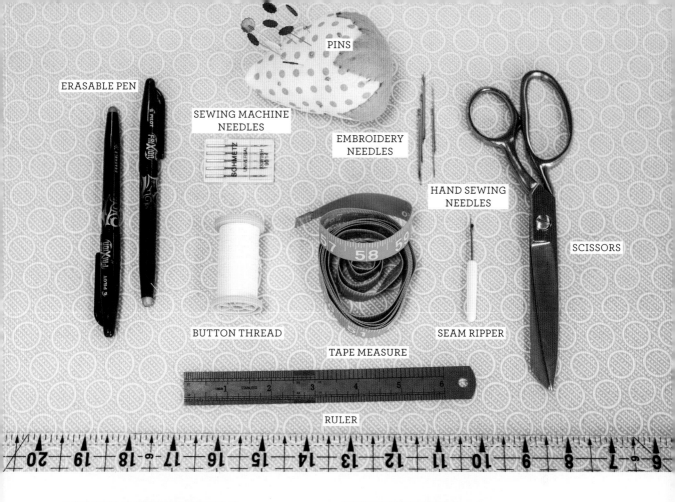

PINS

ERASABLE PEN

SEWING MACHINE
NEEDLES

EMBROIDERY
NEEDLES

HAND SEWING
NEEDLES

SCISSORS

BUTTON THREAD

TAPE MEASURE

SEAM RIPPER

RULER

EMBROIDERY NEEDLES

Embroidery needles are usually a little thicker and have a larger eye, making them easier to thread embroidery floss or perle cotton.

THREAD

Keep a variety of colors on hand.

BUTTON THREAD

This is a nice thick and almost unbreakable thread that is handy to have around for attaching buttons and other sewing projects that involve heavier fabric.

ERASABLE PEN

I always have half a dozen of these fantastic pens on hand for marking my fabric. You can write all over your work and then remove the marker with a hot iron. So cool! My faves are Pilot FriXion pens. You'll find them at an office supply store.

TAPE MEASURE

Sometimes you need to measure something super long, so a tape measure is really handy. It's also handy when you're measuring curves and things that are different shapes.

⁞ Choosing Your Fabrics

Choosing fabric is the most fun part of embarking on a new project. Your fabric choice can really help you create an individual and creative project that will be sure to wow everyone.

There are so many places to find fun fabrics. Fabric stores always have the very best selection, but you would be surprised how many fabrics you can find just lying around the house. Old clothes and thrift shop finds can provide a ton of fun fabrics for these projects. I just love the look of vintage floral sheets reused in fun projects!

COTTON

Cotton is a great weight, is easily washable, and comes in a zillion different prints. I really love to work with quilting cotton. Some of the projects in this book require a heavier cotton fabric like cotton canvas or decorator-weight cotton. I like to use heavier fabric for bags and pillows; it helps a project hold its shape a little better.

FELT

Felt is just about the best fabric to work with. It comes in tons of lovely colors, and the best part is that it doesn't fray. You can make the cutest flowers and shapes from it!

I love to use wool felt, but you can use any kind of felt you can find in the arts and crafts store.

✦ TIP

Turn the iron down if you are ironing synthetic felt. It is made from plastic bottles, which means it will melt if the iron is too hot. It sometimes helps to lay a piece of fabric over the felt to protect it from the hot iron.

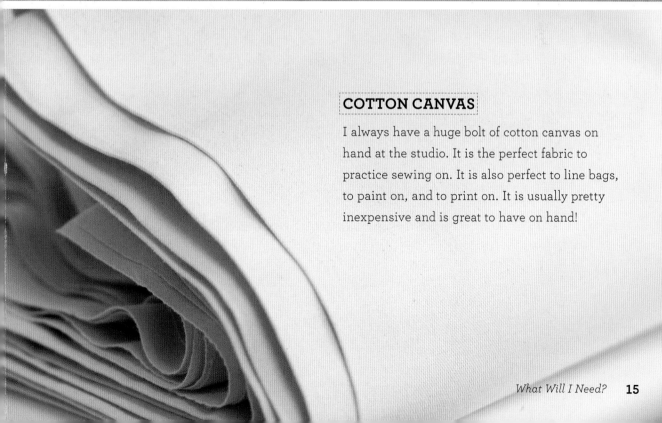

COTTON CANVAS

I always have a huge bolt of cotton canvas on hand at the studio. It is the perfect fabric to practice sewing on. It is also perfect to line bags, to paint on, and to print on. It is usually pretty inexpensive and is great to have on hand!

¡ All About Your Sewing Machine

Sewing on a machine may seem a little ominous or scary; it is a piece of machinery, after all. I am here to tell you that with a little practice, you will be sewing like a pro. It's kind of like driving a car; you need to be able to control the speed and sew in a straight line! Pull out the manual and settle in for a good read. Your manual will explain all about the dials and stitches on your machine—how fun!

✷ TIP

Not sure you'll remember all the bits and pieces on your machine? Grab a piece of decal paper and make your own homemade stickers for your machine. Stick one at each of the threading points to remind you how to thread the machine. When you feel confident about how to use your machine, you can remove the stickers without too much trouble.

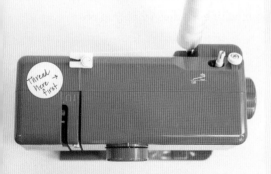

THREADING THE SEWING MACHINE

Most modern machines are threaded in a similar way, usually from right to left. However, if you have an older machine, the threading may be completely different. This is a good time to check the manual.

Believe it or not, if one little section of your machine is not threaded correctly, it will make your thread into a knotted crazy mess. Take the time to really practice threading. You will be glad you did!

SEWING MACHINE NEEDLES

Always make sure that you are fully stocked with universal sewing machine needles. Sometimes your sewing machine needle will break! You may accidentally run over a pin or sew through something a little thick for your machine. There is nothing worse than running out of sewing machine needles when you are in the middle of a project.

To change the needle, loosen the little screw right beside the needle. You usually won't need a screwdriver for this. Remove the old needle and replace it with a new one. Tighten the screw so it is super-duper tight.

¡The Parts of Your Sewing Machine

We use simple sewing machines in the Little Pincushion classroom. Your machine at home may look similar. You are probably pretty familiar with most of the parts already, but I thought I would explain each one to you.

Tension control This is really important. This dial controls the tension or tightness of the top thread. Usually if your stitching looks a little strange, it is because of the tension. Look at your manual or ask an adult for help if you are confused.

Stitch length selector This is the dial you turn to choose how long your stitch length will be. A stitch length of 2.5 is a good standard setting for your machine. Your machine may have a different number or dial; play around with it to find a good even-sized stitch, not too big and not too small. Sometimes there is just a dial with different stitch lengths to choose from. You should turn it to a medium-sized stitch.

Handwheel This round wheel at the end of the machine is the way to manually lift the needle up and down.

Thread take-up lever This part of the machine helps you keep the correct thread tension as you sew. If your machine is not sewing properly or makes a loud thumping sound, it may be because the thread has become unthreaded from the take-up lever.

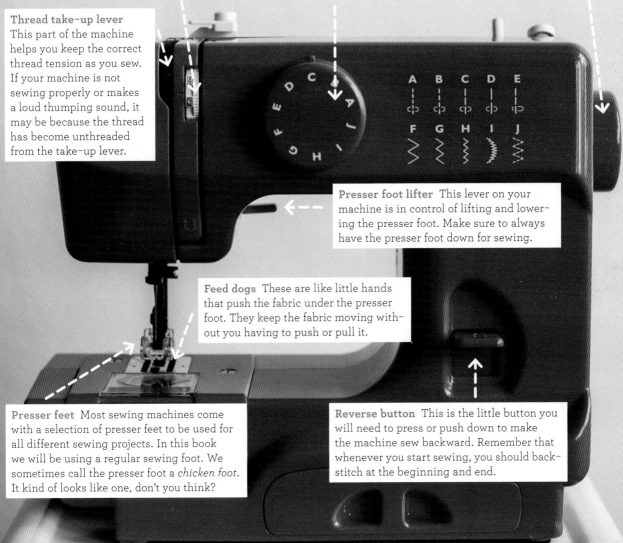

Presser foot lifter This lever on your machine is in control of lifting and lowering the presser foot. Make sure to always have the presser foot down for sewing.

Feed dogs These are like little hands that push the fabric under the presser foot. They keep the fabric moving without you having to push or pull it.

Presser feet Most sewing machines come with a selection of presser feet to be used for all different sewing projects. In this book we will be using a regular sewing foot. We sometimes call the presser foot a *chicken foot*. It kind of looks like one, don't you think?

Reverse button This is the little button you will need to press or push down to make the machine sew backward. Remember that whenever you start sewing, you should backstitch at the beginning and end.

Special Skills

You will notice that at the beginning of most of these projects, there is a little section called "Special Skills." These are skills that you may not have yet, such as using a hot glue gun, using an iron, or using pattern pieces. This is a good time to ask a grown-up for a little help!

Using Pins

It is super important to know how to use pins correctly. Pins are a really big part of making your project look neat and even. Pins hold two (or more) pieces of fabric together so that they don't move when you sew.

My favorite way to pin is with the pins perpendicular to the edge of the fabric. I prefer it this way because the pins are easier to remove as I sew along!

Sewing Around a Corner

Most projects in this book will require you to sew around a corner at some point. It is important to learn how to do this correctly so that your corners always look nice and neat!

1 Sew down the side of your work and stop approximately a presser foot's width from the corner.

2 Turn the handwheel so that your needle is down in the fabric.

3 Lift the presser foot and turn the fabric so that the presser foot is facing in the correct direction to sew the next edge.

4 Make sure that you do this for all your corners. I promise it will make your work look super awesome!

Making and Using Templates

Some of the projects in this book have patterns that you will need to trace to make templates. The project instructions will tell you where in the book to find the patterns.

You will need to enlarge some of the patterns on a photocopier. The percentage to enlarge is on the pattern. Ask an adult to help you if you are not sure how to do this. Other pattern pieces are just the right size for you to trace and use. Some of them may need to be joined together with tape, as they are a little large to fit on one page.

I love to copy my pattern pieces by tracing on tracing paper or parchment paper. You could even use white paper from your home printer. Tracing paper can be found at any arts and crafts store. If you don't already have parchment paper in your kitchen, you will find it in the grocery store near the aluminum foil. If your paper isn't big enough, tape a few pieces together to make a larger piece.

1 Lay the paper over the pattern piece and trace the shape with a pencil. Make sure to add all the markings, like the no-sew zone and other placement marks.

2 Cut out the shape with paper scissors.

3 Pin the tracing-paper pattern shape to the fabric and cut around it with fabric scissors.

You could also trace around the shape with an erasable marker and then cut it out!

Using an Iron

Ironing your project is the perfect way to make it look polished and finished. There is nothing worse than a wrinkled project after all that hard work you put in sewing.

1. Make sure that you ask an adult to supervise when you iron for the first time. Be sure to keep your body and your fingers out of the way when you are ironing.

2. Pay special attention to the fabric you are using. You will see that the iron has different settings for different fabrics. An iron on a hot cotton setting will melt a synthetic fabric.

3. Never leave the iron with the soleplate down on your fabric.

4. Always turn off your iron when you are finished.

-------------->

As long as you pay attention to the settings, you should have no problem.

Sometimes steam can cause a nasty burn, so I like to turn off the steam and keep a little water spray bottle close by; I spray water on the fabric before ironing for a nice and super-smooth look. Most irons have a button to push to turn off the steam. Ask a grown-up to show you. All irons are a little bit different!

Using Paper-Backed Fusible Web

Fusible web is a wonderful product to use when you need to attach one fabric to another without having to pin. It is great for holding felt and fabric shapes in place until you are able to sew. I use paper-backed fusible web all the time. Heat*n*Bond Lite is my all-time favorite. It lets you sew without gumming up your needle.

1 Trace or draw the shape you need on the paper side of the fusible web.

2 Turn off the steam on your iron.

3 Place the bumpy, fusible side down on the wrong side of the fabric and iron.

4 When the fabric has cooled, cut out the shape.

5 Peel off the backing paper.

6 Position the shape on the fabric and iron it in place.

7 Sew nice and neatly around the shape. Use an erasable pen to draw a stitch line if you need to.

Making a Pom-Pom

↑ **1** Wrap yarn around the widest part of your hand about 75 times (or more for a bigger pom).

↑ **2** Carefully slide the yarn off your hand, keeping the yarn together in a neat bundle.

3 Cut another piece of yarn and tie it around the middle of the yarn bundle. Make sure that the loops are free for trimming.

↑ **4** Tie it super tight in a double knot.

5 Snip the loops with a sharp pair of scissors.

↑ **6** Give the pom-pom an allover haircut until it is the size that you like.

Using a Hot Glue Gun

Hot glue guns are so awesome! But, yes, they are pretty darn hot. Always make sure you are using a low-temp glue gun. They usually have it written on the package at the store.

Always ask an adult before you use one and make sure to have a little bowl of ice water on hand in case of a burn.

Using a Staple Gun

Have you ever used a staple gun before? I am sure you have seen an adult using one. Well, great news! With a bit of help and supervision, you can be using a staple gun like a pro!

WHAT YOU NEED TO KNOW

- Always ask an adult for help.

- Make sure you are using the correct staples to fit your gun. There are many different sizes to choose from. (Your box will tell you what size staples you need.)

- Never use a staple gun unless it is face-down. Some power guns have a safety mechanism that will stop the gun from working unless it is pressed down on a surface.

- Use firm pressure when using a staple gun. If you have trouble with this, ask a grown-up for help.

TIP

Never use a staple gun without adult supervision. They are awesome tools but can be dangerous if not used correctly.

Sewing on a Button

After years of teaching kids just like you, I am always surprised how many of them are afraid of sewing on a button. It is really super simple and can make your project look extra awesome! Have you seen how many amazing buttons there are out there? I have been collecting pretty ones for years.

1 Mark the spot for your button.

2 Thread a needle with button thread or embroidery floss. Tie a knot in the end of the thread.

3 Hold the button on the fabric at the spot where you marked. Bring the needle up from behind the fabric and through a hole in the button.

4 Pull the needle all the way through the hole and then push the needle down to the back of the fabric through the hole beside the one you just came through.

5 Bring the needle back up from behind the fabric and through the hole and then down again just like before.

6 Repeat this a couple more times until the button feels tight and secure.

↑ ⑦ Bring the needle up from behind the fabric but do not push it through the buttonhole. Instead, push it between the fabric and button and wrap the thread around underneath the button 3 or 4 times. This helps your button to be secure!

↑ ⑧ Push the needle back down to the back of the fabric and secure it with a double knot.

Trim the thread.

Hand Sewing

Hand sewing is the perfect technique to make your machine-sewn project look even better and craftier. It's easy to get used to working on only a sewing machine, and the less time you spend on hand sewing, the more challenging it will seem. Here's the great news: it's really, really easy and fun!

Our projects will require only a few kinds of hand stitches.

SEWING A RUNNING STITCH

Running stitch is probably the simplest hand stitch. It is basically just an up-and-down stitch.

↑ ① Knot the end of the thread.

↑ ② Push the needle up from underneath the fabric.

  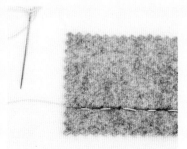

↑ ③ Push the needle down approximately ¼″ away from where you brought it up. Refer to the tip (below) to make it easier to sew even stitches.

↑ ④ Bring the needle up again another ¼″ away and then push it down again, keeping your stitches as even as possible.

↑ ⑤ Continue sewing like this all the way around your project.

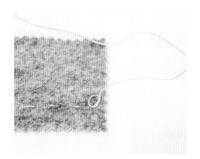 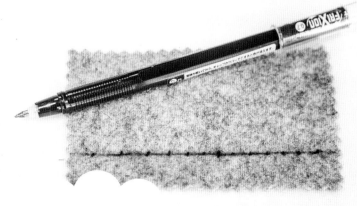

↑ ⑥ When you get to the end, make sure your final stitch ends on the back of the fabric. Tie a knot in the thread nice and close to the fabric.

✦TIP

It can be really helpful to use an erasable pen and draw dots on your fabric ¼″ apart to use as a stitch guide. These dots can help you keep your stitches neat and even and can be removed with a hot iron.

SEWING A WHIPSTITCH

Whipstitch is an easy stitch that is used to close holes on things like pillows and soft toys.

1 Push the needle through both sides of the fabric opening and tie a double knot in the thread.

2 Bring the needle up through one side and out the other side of the fabric.

3 Move a little below and push the needle through both sides of the opening. Pull the stitch nice and tight so that the sides of the opening come together.

4 Don't forget to tie a knot when you are finished.

SEWING A BACKSTITCH

I love to use backstitch with embroidery floss or perle cotton when I am embroidering letters or words. It makes a pretty, continuous line that looks good even around curves.

1 Bring the needle up from behind the fabric.

2 Push it down again at the next dot.

3 Instead of continuing like a running stitch and sewing the stitch forward, you will bring the needle up ¼˝ away and then push it back down in the hole of the last stitch you made.

4 So basically you move forward and then stitch backward. It makes a nice continuous line without the spaces of a running stitch.

SEWING A VICKI KNOT

There is a traditional embroidery stitch known as the French knot. I have always found it a little tricky to teach to children. Lucky for me, my friend Vicki taught me her own variation, known as the Vicki knot. I am excited to share it with you!

1 Knot the end of an arm's-length piece of embroidery floss or perle cotton.

Note *An arm's length of thread is measured from your fingertips to your shoulder. This makes the thread piece easy to manage.*

2 Thread the embroidery needle and bring the needle through the fabric from behind on a marked spot.

3 Tie a knot in your thread, but before you tighten the knot, place the tip of your needle in the center of the knot.

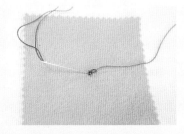

4 Ease the knot down the needle until it is right on top of the fabric.

6 Push the needle through to the back of the fabric and secure with a knot.

7 If you want a larger knot, tie a second knot in Steps 3–5 and treat both knots as one in Step 6.

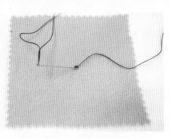

5 Tighten the knot.

Sewing Terms

*There may be some words in these projects that you have never heard before.
Never fear. I am here to explain them all to you!*

LEAVE A TAIL

One of the most annoying things that happens to my students in class is when the sewing machine repeatedly becomes unthreaded. It takes time to have to constantly rethread your machine when all you really want to do is sew, sew, sew! I have an easy tip so that does not happen to you. Pull out an 8˝-long "tail" of machine and bobbin thread before you begin sewing. That way, when the machine needle goes down, it won't take your thread with it.

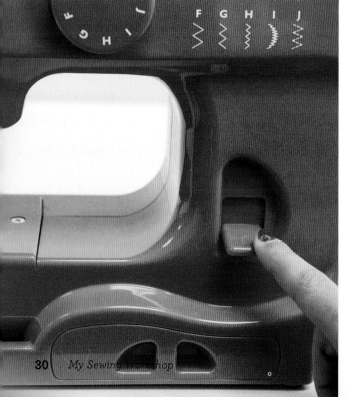

BACKSTITCH

It is important to backstitch at the beginning and end of every stitch line. Backstitching just creates a strong beginning and ending that prevents your stitching from coming undone. Most machines have a reverse button or lever that you will need to hold down to go backward. Take a look at your machine manual to find it.

When you start sewing a seam, sew a few stitches forward and then hold down the reverse button for a few stitches. Now let go of the button and continue forward until the end of the seam. When you get to the end of the seam, hold down the reverse button again to secure the stitches.

EDGE OF THE PRESSER FOOT ON THE EDGE OF THE FABRIC

Many sewing machines come with a regular presser foot that is ⅜˝ from the center to the edge. For that reason, these projects use a ⅜˝ seam allowance. That means that most of the projects can simply be sewn with the edge of the foot on the edge of the fabric!

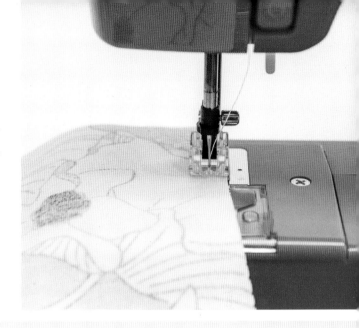

FAT QUARTER

A fat quarter is a quarter of a yard, but it is not a regular quarter-yard, which is 9˝ × 44˝; it has a different shape. In order to get a fat quarter of fabric, you would divide one yard of quilting fabric into four large rectangles, so each rectangle measures 18˝ × 22˝.

Fat quarters are great because you can actually get more out of this measurement than with a regular quarter-yard. If you go to your local fabric store, you can usually find stacks of fat quarters by the shelves of quilt fabric. What's great is that they are inexpensive and a great way to add fabric variety to your projects!

NO-SEW ZONE

You may come across the term "no-sew zone" in this book. This is my own made-up term for the area where you don't sew … you know, when you are sewing a piece that needs to have an opening so it can be turned right side out.

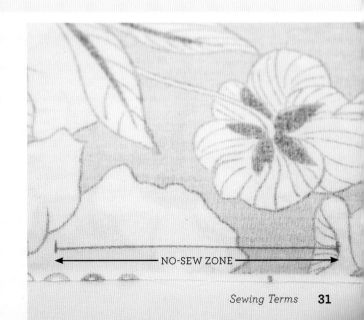

NO-SEW ZONE

WRONG SIDE

RIGHT SIDE

RIGHT SIDES TOGETHER

It is important to sew with right sides together. This means that you match up the fabrics with the pretty (right) sides facing each other, and you sew on the wrong side. That way, when you turn your project right side out, there will be no messy raw edges showing.

SEAM

This is the stitching line you have sewn to join one piece of fabric to another piece of fabric.

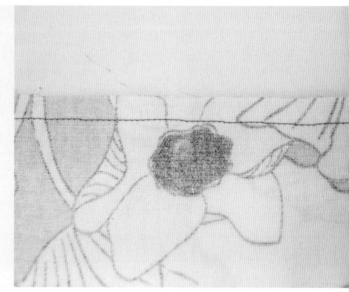

SEAM ALLOWANCE

This is the measurement from the edge of the fabric to the stitch line. The seam allowance for most of the projects in this book is ⅜˝. If your presser foot only measures ¼˝, you could use a piece of washi or masking tape as a guide. Place the inner edge of the tape ⅜˝ out from the machine's needle. Sew with the edge of the fabric on the edge of the masking tape. I think it really helps when you have some way to line everything up.

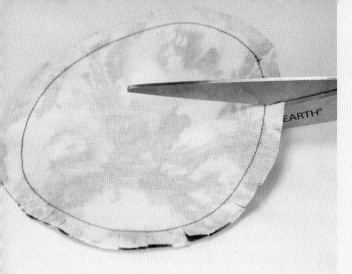

CLIP THE CURVES

Sometimes when you are sewing something that has curves and needs to be turned right side out, you need to clip the curves so that the curves stay nice and curvy.

When you have finished sewing a curvy seam, use a sharp pair of scissors to carefully clip the fabric every inch. Make sure not to clip the stitching!

TOPSTITCH

Sew a straight stitch to give your work a neat, finished look. It is usually a line sewn between ⅛″ and ¼″ from the edge around the outside of a completed project.

If you feel worried about creating a neat stitch, you can draw the line with a removable-ink pen first and then sew on that line.

TOPSTITCH

Do You Feel Confident?

So, now you are ready to set off and start sewing some of the projects from this book for all your family, friends, and pets!

> **Threading your machine and bobbin?**

> **Sewing with the edge of the presser foot on the edge of the fabric?**

> **Sewing a straight line?**

> **Pivoting around corners?**

> **Using pins correctly?**

If you answered "No" to any of these questions, go back to the previous sections in the book and take a little more time. Ask for help!

Not Your Grandma's Doily Tank

How adorable is this tank top with that hand-dyed doily gorgeousness? This is such an easy and fun project. You'll have to make one for each of your friends!

> What Do I Need?

- Plain colored tank top
- Crocheted doily (Find it in a craft store or thrift shop.)
- Fabric dye (I use Rit dye from the supermarket.)
- Double-sided fusible web (measuring a little larger than the doily) (Refer to Using Paper-Backed Fusible Web, page 22.)
- Apron or old clothes
- Rubber gloves
- Wooden spoon
- Old plastic dishpan
- Measuring cup
- Sewing machine
- Basic supplies (page 12)

> Special Skills

- Refer to The Rules of Sewing (page 9)
- Using fusible web (page 22)
- Using an iron (page 21)

Dyeing the Doily

You can dye your doily in a color to match the tank top. Or choose any color you like. First, put on your apron or old clothes, please! And ask an adult for setup and dyeing help.

⭐TIP Make Extras!

As long as you are mixing dye, you might want to dye several doilies. Then you'll have some ready for making more tops!

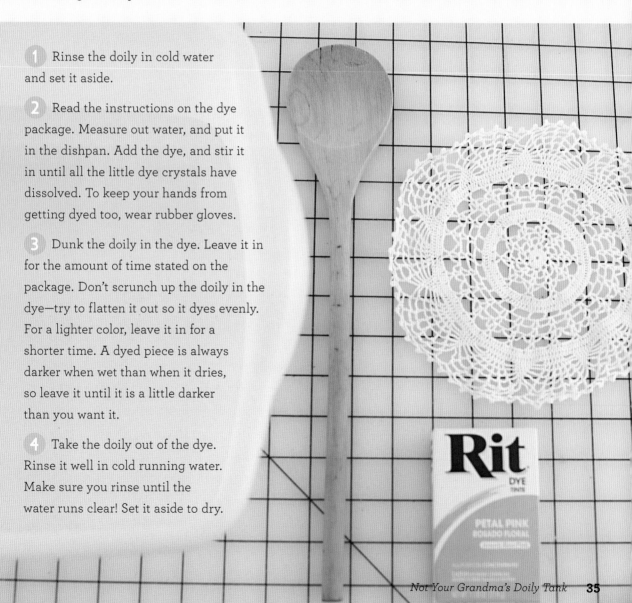

1 Rinse the doily in cold water and set it aside.

2 Read the instructions on the dye package. Measure out water, and put it in the dishpan. Add the dye, and stir it in until all the little dye crystals have dissolved. To keep your hands from getting dyed too, wear rubber gloves.

3 Dunk the doily in the dye. Leave it in for the amount of time stated on the package. Don't scrunch up the doily in the dye—try to flatten it out so it dyes evenly. For a lighter color, leave it in for a shorter time. A dyed piece is always darker when wet than when it dries, so leave it until it is a little darker than you want it.

4 Take the doily out of the dye. Rinse it well in cold running water. Make sure you rinse until the water runs clear! Set it aside to dry.

¡ Let's Make It!

↑ **1** Place the dry doily on the paper side of the fusible web. Trace around the doily.

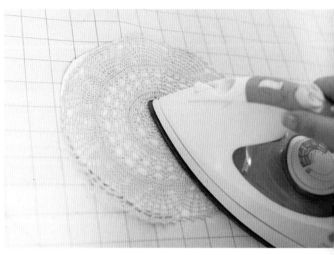

↑ **2** Cut out the circle. Position the circle of fusible web with the rough side facing up, and iron the doily onto the circle.

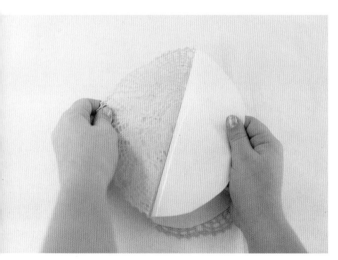

↑ **3** Peel off the backing paper.

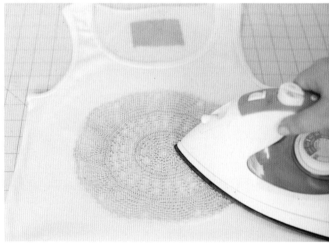

↑ **4** Center the doily on your tank top, sticky side down, and iron.

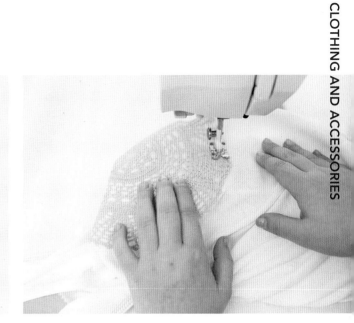

★ TIP Make It Yours!

I like the look of the centered doily. But you can iron it on anywhere you want. You could even add more than one doily to your tank top. Remember, this is your project!

5 Now we'll sew the doily to the tank top. Carefully slide the tank top under your sewing machine presser foot. Make sure that only the tank front is under the foot. You don't want to sew the front and back together! Line up the edge of the doily with the edge of the foot. You'll find that the doily is a little bit lumpy and bumpy. Sew slowly, and just do your best to sew evenly. When you're done, trim all the threads.

Marvel at the gorgeous tank top you just created. It's one of a kind!

Super-Simple Skirt

*What's more fun than a skirt you made yourself? It's pretty hard
to stop at just one. Let your inner fashion designer take this basic
pattern and make it your own. Add some pom-poms or stitch on some
trim. You could even add a pocket.*

> What Do I Need?

- Printed quilting cotton
  fabric (The amount of
  fabric will depend on your
  measurements. See Prepare
  the Pieces, Steps 1 and 2,
  next page, to figure this
  out.)

- 1 yard of 2˝-wide knitted
  elastic (I like black, but you
  can use any color.)

- Sewing machine

- Basic supplies (page 12)

> Special Skills

- Refer to The Rules of
  Sewing (page 9)

- Using an iron (page 21)

Prepare the Pieces

Wash your cotton fabric in warm water. Dry it in the dryer. If it's going to shrink, you want that to happen before you start cutting and sewing. That way, your wonderful skirt will still fit you no matter how many times you wash it!

★TIP Measure First!

Don't buy any fabric until you have checked your measurements! You may need more fabric if your waist measurement (doubled) is larger than the width of the fabric. Read the steps for measuring.

1 Take your measurements with a measuring tape. This is easiest with a partner. Measure your waist at the point where the waistband will sit. Make sure it's not too low on your hips. Write down your measurement on paper.

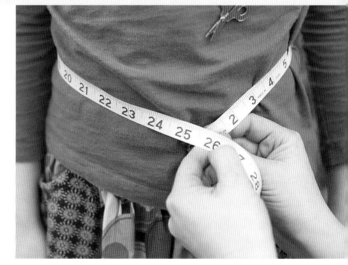

2 Take 2 times your waist measurement to get the amount of fabric you need to buy. For example, if your waist measures 24˝, you will buy 48˝ of fabric. (You can't buy exactly 48˝ of fabric, but you can buy 1⅜ yards, which is 49½˝ of fabric—close enough.) No more cutting is needed for the width of the skirt, except to straighten the ends of the fabric.

3 Measure how long you would like your skirt to be. This skirt looks best a little above the knee. Make a note of that measurement.

----

4 Add 2″ to your skirt length measurement from Step 3. Measure and cut your skirt fabric to this length. When you measure the fabric, make sure that you have the selvage running down the side or length of your fabric piece. Make sure to cut as straight as you can. I usually use a ruler and a disappearing-ink marker for this part!

5 Subtract 2″ from your waist measurement from Step 1. Measure and cut the elastic to this length.

★TIP Leftover Fabric

You will have a long strip of leftover fabric after you cut out your skirt. Use it to make another project—such as a matching Blossoming Necklace (page 51), a Cross-Body Handy Pouch (page 78), or a cute Super-Secret Journal Cover (page 126). You could even make a little something for your BFF. It's fun to be creative with fabric leftovers!

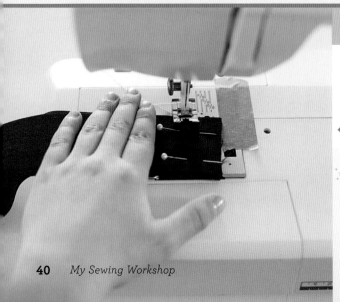

¡ Let's Make It!

1 Fold the elastic in half, and line up the 2 raw ends. Sew the ends together with a 1″ seam allowance.

★TIP Mark the Spot

You can make it super easy to sew a 1″ seam. Measure 1″ to the right from your sewing machine needle. Stick down a small piece of blue painter's tape. Use this as a guide. Then just pull off the tape when you're finished.

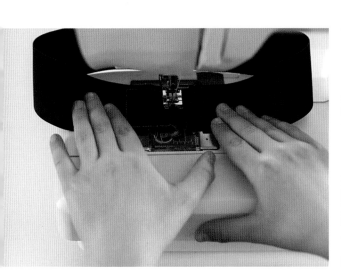

↑ **2** Open out and flatten the ends of the elastic. Sew around the opened-out edges in a square. (Look at the picture for Step 5, below, to see the finished square.)

↑ **3** Fold your skirt piece in half with right sides together. Carefully match up the edges. Pin it down the length of the fabric.

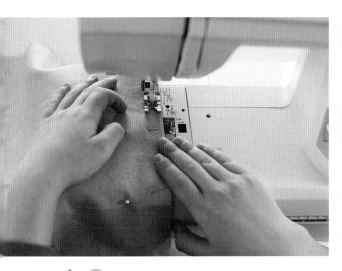

↑ **4** Sew down the side, with the edge of the presser foot on the edge of the fabric. When you are done, iron down the seam you have just sewn, just to make it lovely and flat.

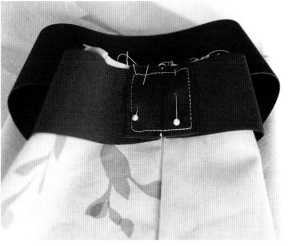

↑ **5** Now attach the elastic. Turn the skirt right side out. Line up the elastic seam with the skirt seam. Line up the edge of the elastic with the raw edge around the skirt top.

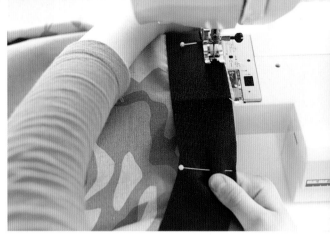

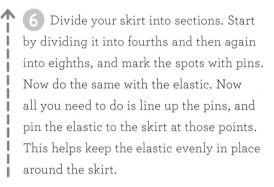

6 Divide your skirt into sections. Start by dividing it into fourths and then again into eighths, and mark the spots with pins. Now do the same with the elastic. Now all you need to do is line up the pins, and pin the elastic to the skirt at those points. This helps keep the elastic evenly in place around the skirt.

7 There's a little trick to sewing elastic. Sew with the edge of the presser foot on the edge of the elastic. Hold on to the elastic and fabric from behind the presser foot with your left hand. At the same time, hold the elastic and fabric in front with your right hand, and pull it taut as you sew. This helps everything stay flat instead of bunching up. Finish with a backstitch.

*TIP

If you have a sewing machine with a button that makes the needle end in the down position when you stop sewing, now would be the time to press that button. If your machine doesn't have it, make sure that every time you stop the sewing machine, the needle is down in the fabric.

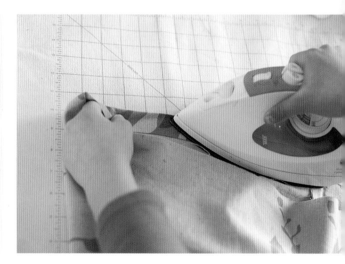

8 Now you're ready to hem your skirt. Try it on, just to be sure that it will be the right length with a 2″ hem. To create the hem, fold up the bottom 1″. Iron it flat. Then fold up the hem 1″, and iron it again.

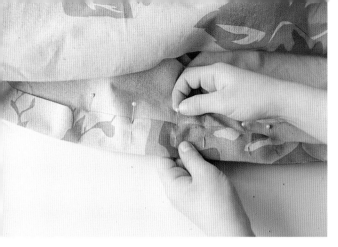

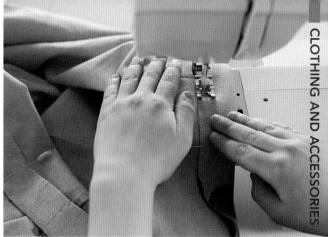

↑ **9** Pin the hem in place.

↑ **10** With the edge of the presser foot on the edge of the folded fabric, sew as straight as you can all the way around the hem. Remember to backstitch. When you are done, trim your threads.

Turn your skirt right side out.

Hooray—you're finished!

Be sure to tell everyone that you made it!

DIY Fabric Design

Why not be creative and print your own fabric? You could tie-dye a piece of cloth, draw a design with fabric markers—the options are endless. Here I'll show you how to stencil on fabric. This project uses a ready-made bag. But you can do the same thing on a piece of fabric. Then sew it up into anything that tickles your fancy!

You will need freezer paper to make your stencil. You can find it at any grocery store, or you can get sheets of it from C&T Publishing. Freezer paper has a shiny, waxy side that can be stuck temporarily to fabric using an iron.

> What Do I Need?

You'll need the heart pattern (page 228).

- Fabric paints (I like DecoArt SoSoft Fabric Acrylics.)
- Paint tray, old plate, or even a paper plate
- Plain canvas tote bag
- Freezer paper
- Craft knife
- Self-healing cutting mat
- Stencil brush (You can either use one with bristles, or you can use one with a sponge on the end.)
- Pencil

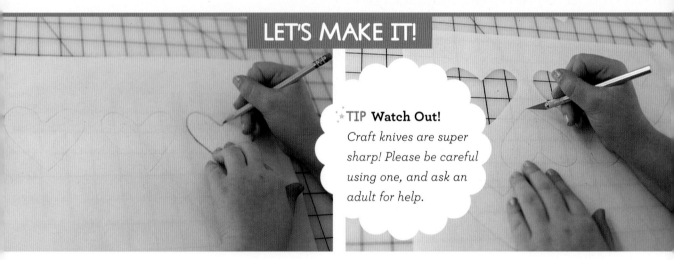

LET'S MAKE IT!

*★TIP **Watch Out!***
Craft knives are super sharp! Please be careful using one, and ask an adult for help.

1. Cut a piece of freezer paper the size of the print area you need. Draw your design on the nonshiny side. Leave plenty of space around the edges of your design. With a repeat pattern like the one shown here, make sure that your shapes are not too close together.

2. Very carefully use a craft knife to cut out your shapes. You should not need to press very hard. Be sure to use a cutting mat under the freezer paper. Otherwise, the knife will cut into your table! That would be really, really bad, so be careful.

3 Iron your tote bag nice and smooth. Center the freezer paper on the bag, with the shiny side facing down. Very carefully iron the paper onto the fabric so it sticks. Make sure that every little corner is firmly stuck. If the paper is not stuck down properly, the paint may bleed under the stencil and mess up your fab design!

4 Apply a thin layer of paint with the stencil brush. Use only a small amount of paint so it doesn't run. Dab the brush with an up-and-down motion.

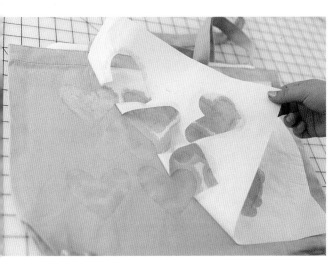

5 Wait a couple of hours until the paint is dry to the touch. Then peel off the paper. Ta-da!

Hang the piece outside or in a warm spot in your house for a day or two to let it dry completely. Iron over your design to set the paint. Now you will be able to wash your piece if you accidentally have a spill!

Blooming Headband

Don't flowers just make you happy? Imagine how happy you'll be when you're wearing a little bit of springtime happiness on your head!

> What Do I Need?

- Piece of felt at least 4″ × 20″ in your favorite color for the flower
- Piece of green felt at least 5″ × 5″ for the leaves
- Plain headband
- Several seed beads
- Hot glue gun and glue stick
- Basic supplies (page 12)

> Special Skills

- Refer to The Rules of Sewing (page 9)
- Making and using templates (page 20)
- Hand sewing (page 26)
- Using a hot glue gun (page 23)

Prepare the Pieces

You'll need the leaf and circle patterns (page 228).

1. Cut a strip of felt 4″ × 18″ for a larger flower. Or cut it 3″ × 18″ for a slightly smaller flower.

2. Trace the circle pattern. Cut 1 circle out of the same color felt as your flower.

3. Trace the leaf pattern. Cut 2 leaves from green felt.

Let's Make It!

↑ 1 Fold the strip of felt in half. Pin it to hold the fold in place.

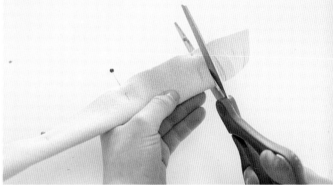

↑ 2 With scissors, cut even slits about ¼″ apart in the folded edge. Be careful so you stop cutting ¼″–½″ from the opposite edge. Cut slits along the entire strip.

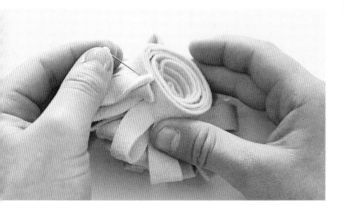

↑ 3 Take out the pins, and very carefully roll up the strip as tightly as you can. Pin the end of the strip to hold it in place.

TIP Glue It!
You can do this part with hot glue. But sewing gives the flower the fullness it needs to look flowertastic!

4 Thread a needle with button thread and knot the end of the thread. Begin from the center, and push the needle through all the layers to the outside of the flower. Push the needle back through the center and then through the layers again to a point about ¼″ away from where you sewed it the first time. Keep sewing back through the center and then through the layers, moving around the circle with each stitch. As you sew, the thread will make a kind of star pattern holding everything together. Pull the thread nice and tight after each stitch.

5 Finish by tying a knot in the thread.

6 Use your fingers to fluff out the flower to the desired fabulousness.

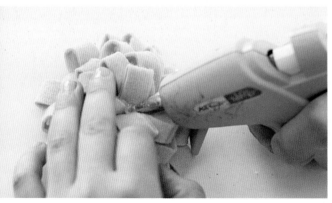

7 Add a dab of hot glue in the center of the flower.

8 Drop in a couple of seed beads for extra va-va-voom.

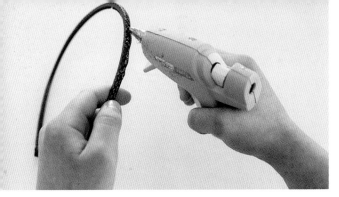

⬆ ⑨ Decide where the flower will be on the headband. Slightly to the side seems to look the best. With your hot glue gun, carefully run a bead of glue along the headband. Make it about the length of the leaf.

⬆ ⑩ Attach the leaf. Now do the same with the other leaf.

⬆ ⑪ Put a big dab of glue on both the flower and the felt circle.

⬆ ⑫ Carefully press the flower onto the headband, with the circle on the underside of the band. This will hold the flower and headband together nice and tight! Wait a few minutes for it to dry completely.

Pom-Pom Earrings

These seriously cute pom-tastic earrings will have you feeling warm and fuzzy all over!

> What Do I Need?

Makes 1 pair.

- 2 tiny matching pom-poms or small felted balls (Find these in all sizes at a craft or hobby store.)

- Earring post findings (Find these in the jewelry-making section of a craft supply store.)

- Hot glue gun and glue stick

> Special Skills

- Refer to The Rules of Sewing (page 9)

- Using a hot glue gun (page 23)

¡ Let's Make It!

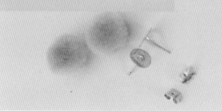

↑ ① Take off the earring backs, and lay out the pieces.

↑ ② Put a dab of glue on the cup of the earring piece. Add the pom-pom, and hold it in place for a minute or 2. Repeat with the other earring.

A TEENY BIT MORE CHALLENGING

Blossoming Necklace

This cute necklace makes me think of long, warm summer days. It's kind of like wearing a garden around your neck (without the bugs, of course!).

Finished length: About 48˝

What Do I Need?

- ¼ yard of bright quilting cotton
- ¼ yard of plain or printed quilting cotton for the flowers
- Large bag of ½˝ plastic craft beads
- Chopstick or knitting needle for turning your work
- Sewing machine
- Basic supplies (page 12)

Special Skills

- Refer to The Rules of Sewing (page 9)
- Making and using templates (page 20)
- Hand sewing (page 26)
- Using an iron (page 21)
- Sewing around a corner (page 19)

Prepare the Pieces

You'll need the flower pattern (page 228).

1 Decide how many flowers you want. You will be making clusters of flowers. Each cluster works best with about 6 flowers. I like to use 4-6 clusters of flowers on a necklace. But it's really up to you.

2 Use the pattern to cut out all your flowers from the quilting cotton.

3 Cut 2 strips 3˝ × the width of the fabric for the necklace.

- →

Let's Make It!

1 Fold a flower into fourths by folding it in half and then in half again. Iron it. Repeat for all the flowers. Set them aside.

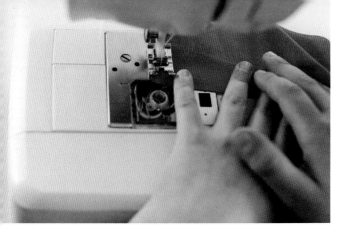 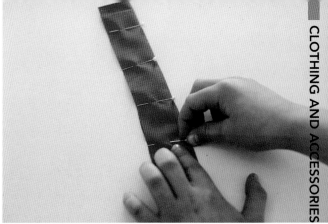

↑ **②** Sew the 2 strips of fabric together end to end to create a super-long strip. Measure the strip, and cut it at 60˝.

↑ **③** Fold the strip in half along its length, right sides together. Iron it along the fold. Pin all along the open side of the strip.

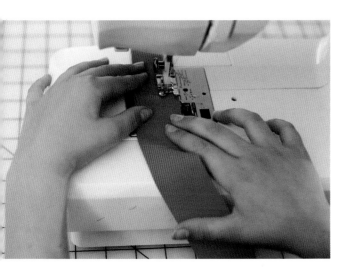 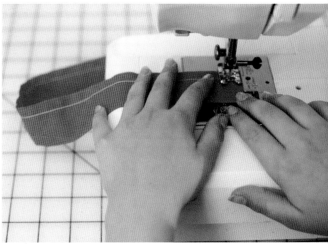

↑ **④** Carefully stitch along the open long side of the strip. Sew with the edge of the presser foot on the edge of the fabric.

↑ **⑤** When you reach the bottom, sew across the short end. Secure with a back-stitch. You should have a long tube with one closed end.

TIP

Thrift shops are a great place to find old bead necklaces just crying out to be cut up and repurposed. Isn't recycling awesome?

Blossoming Necklace   **53**

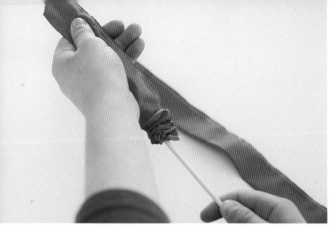

6 Now turn the tube right side out. This looks hard, but it's really not! The secret is a chopstick or knitting needle. Start at the sewn end. Use the chopstick to gently push the end inside itself. As you push the tube right side out, keep pulling down the edges.

7 Use your measuring tape to measure 10˝ from the closed end of the tube. Tie a knot.

TIP How Long?

It's good to leave 10˝ of fabric at each end of your necklace. This way, you can adjust the length when you tie it around your neck.

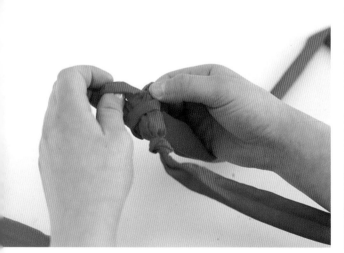

8 Feed a plastic bead down inside the tube to the knot. Now tie a knot in the tube right above the bead. Add a second bead, and tie a knot above it.

9 Keep going until your necklace is the length you want. Tie the final knot. Measure about 10½˝, and cut off the end of the tube.

⬆ ⑩ Fold in ½″ of the open end, and topstitch it closed.

⬆ ⑪ Thread a needle and knot the thread. Stack 6 folded flowers in your hand, with the folded corners on top of each other.

⬆ ⑫ Push the needle through the folded corners of all 6 flowers. Now push the needle through one of the knots between the beads. Push it through a second time.

⬆ ⑬ Tie a knot to secure the thread.

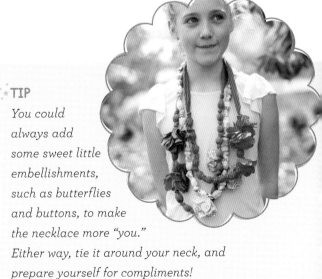

⭐ TIP

You could always add some sweet little embellishments, such as butterflies and buttons, to make the necklace more "you."
Either way, tie it around your neck, and prepare yourself for compliments!

⬆ ⑭ Add as many flower clusters as you want. Remember to tie the thread in a knot at the end of every cluster. That way the flowers won't fall off your necklace.

Blossoming Necklace   **55**

Stitchy Stripy Watchband

You will love telling everyone what time it is with this super-adorable stitched watchband. Wrap it around your wrist a couple of times, or wrap it in some sweet paper as a gift for someone sweet!

> What Do I Need?

- An old watch face with a watchband bar or a watch face from a craft store (I used a watch face with a 1″ bar. The watch bar is the little bar on each side of the watch face where a strap is normally attached. Use a tape measure or ruler to measure the length of the bar; that will help you decide how wide your fabric should be.)

- 4″ × 22″ strip of fun fabric

- 4″ × 22″ strip of featherweight fusible interfacing

- Fun-colored thread to coordinate with the fabric

- Snap kit (which includes a snap tool and size 15 or 16 snaps)

- Hammer (to use with the snap tool)

- Basic supplies (page 12)

> Special Skills

- Refer to The Rules of Sewing (page 9)

- Using an iron (page 21)

¡ Prepare the Pieces

1 Measure your wrist by wrapping the measuring tape around your wrist twice. The watchband will be super long, so you can wrap it around your wrist twice! Decide on a length that is not too tight and will allow the 2 ends to overlap at least 1″ and still feel comfortable. Write down that measurement.

2 Add ½″ to the measurement from Step 1.

3 Cut a strip of fabric and interfacing that is 2″ or 3″ or 4″ wide (refer to the note below) and the length from Step 2.

Note *Cut the fabric strip 4 times as wide as the measurement of the watch bar. For example, you need a width of 4″ for a 1″ watch bar, 3″ for a ¾″ watch bar, and 2″ for a ½″ watch bar.*

¡ Let's Make It!

If you are using a ¼″ presser foot, don't forget to use washi tape as a guide to make the correct seam allowance width for this project (page 32).

1 Use an iron to fuse the interfacing to the back of the fabric strip.

2 Fold in each end ½″ and press with an iron.

3 Fold the strip in half lengthwise, with wrong sides together. Press with an iron.

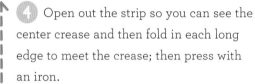 **4** Open out the strip so you can see the center crease and then fold in each long edge to meet the crease; then press with an iron.

5 Refold the strip on the crease, so the raw edges are on the inside, and press really well with an iron.

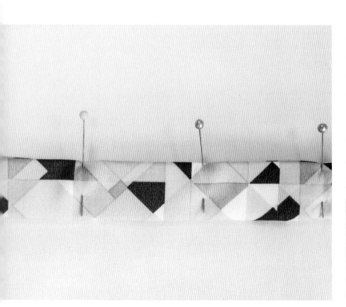

6 Use some pins to hold the strip together while you are sewing.

7 Thread your sewing machine with fun-colored thread and stitch all the way around, nice and close to the edge.

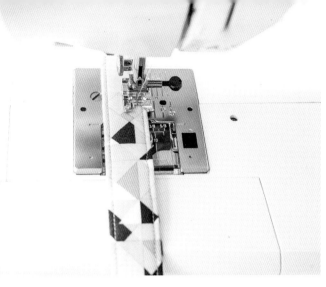

↑ ⑧ Use the sewing machine to sew your own crazy stripes up and down the strip. You could even experiment with some zigzag stripes.

↑ ⑨ Thread the strip through the bars on the watch face.

¡Finish Up!

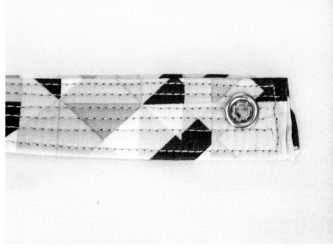

↑ Using a snap-attaching tool and hammer, attach a snap to each end of the band. Make sure to read the instructions on the snap package!

Button Ring

How about a little button bling? Get creative with buttons. Stack them, bedazzle them—the choice is yours. You will be sure to have the most stylish fingers on the block!

> What Do I Need?

Makes 1 ring.

- Buttons (1 small, 1 medium, 1 larger)
- Ring blank (Find this in the jewelry-making section of a craft supply store.)
- Hot glue gun and glue stick

> Special Skills

- Refer to The Rules of Sewing (page 9)
- Using a hot glue gun (page 23)

¡ Let's Make It!

1 Put a dab of hot glue on the back of the medium button. Center it on top of the large button, and press firmly. Then glue the small button on top of that.

------------------------>

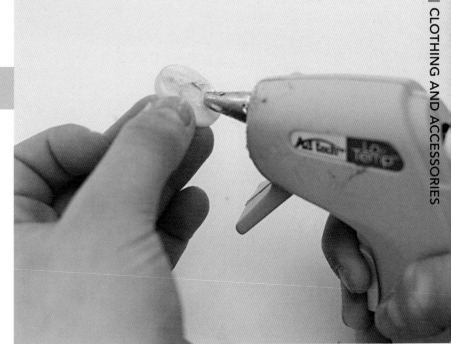

2 Place a big dab of hot glue on the top of your ring blank. Attach the button stack. Press it firmly to make sure it is stuck down really well.

3 Wait a few minutes before wearing your ring. You want the glue to be set and super dry.

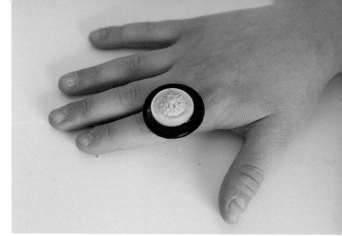

Don't stop with a ring. You can also use this idea to make the cutest barrettes in town!

A TEENY BIT MORE CHALLENGING

Zippy Pouch

I personally can never have enough bags! This little cutie is perfect for carrying everything a girl could possibly need. You could fit your whole lip gloss collection in here! In this project, you'll learn to sew in a zipper.

Finished size: 8½″ × 6½″

❯ What Do I Need?

- ¼ yard of fun printed fabric for the outside
- ¼ yard of fabric for the lining (I used another fun print!)
- 9″ zipper
- Embroidery thread for the zipper pull (*optional*)
- Sewing machine and zipper foot
- Basic supplies (page 12)

❯ Special Skills

- Refer to The Rules of Sewing (page 9)
- Using an iron (page 21)
- Sewing around a corner (page 19)

Prepare the Pieces

1 Cut 2 pieces of printed fabric 7″ × 9″ for the outside bag.

2 Cut 2 pieces of lining fabric 7″ × 9″.

Let's Make It!

1 Lay 1 lining piece and 1 outside bag piece wrong sides together. (We usually do everything with right sides together. Not this time!) Pin them together. This picture shows the outside piece on top.

2 Fold down both layers together ¼″ at the top edge. Fold them onto the lining side. (The photo shows the lining side.) Iron them flat. Do the same thing with the other 2 pieces.

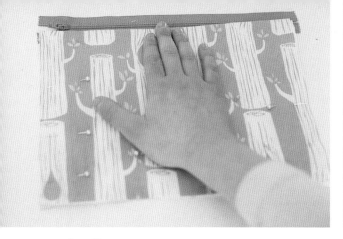

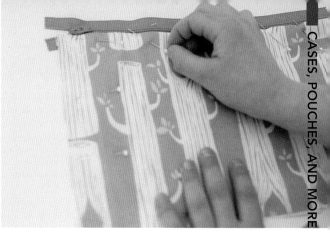

3 Lay the zipper right side up. (The right side of the zipper is the side with the zipper pull on it.) Lay the folded edge of 1 pouch piece, lining side down, over the fabric part of the zipper next to one side of the zipper teeth.

4 Carefully pin the fabric piece to the zipper.

5 Repeat Steps 3 and 4 with the other pouch piece. Pin this piece to the opposite side of the zipper teeth.

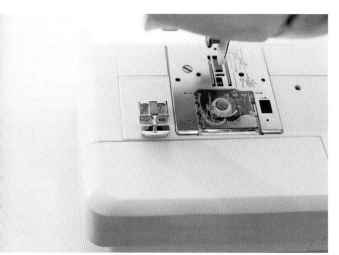

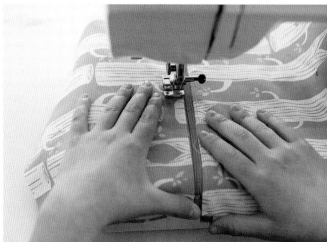

6 Now attach the zipper foot to your sewing machine. This is a good time to pull out your sewing machine manual to see how. Ask an adult for help if you need to! Attach the foot so that the needle is on the right-hand side so it will be close to the zipper teeth when you sew.

7 Carefully sew all the way down both sides of the zipper. Make sure to have the edge of the zipper foot butted up to the edge of the zipper teeth. When you are finished, change back to the regular presser foot.

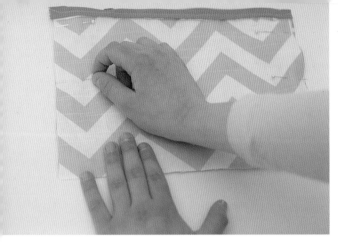

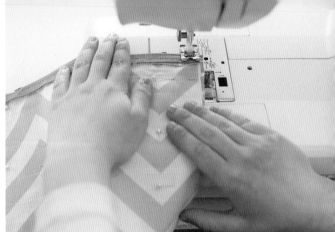

8 Unzip the zipper. You may think that it would be easier to keep the pouch zipped at this point, but you really need to leave it open so you can turn it right side out later. Fold the pouch out so that the right sides are facing. Pin around the sides and bottom.

9 Now sew all 3 sides with the edge of the presser foot on the edge of the fabric. Make sure to start and end with a backstitch.

10 Trim the points off the corners. Don't cut into your stitching! Trim all those pesky threads.

11 Turn the pouch right side out. You may want to iron it, to make it look super sharp!

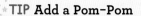

TIP Add a Pom-Pom

Do you want to add a cute pom-pom? Check out the craft section at your local hobby store. You will be amazed at all the fun colors and sizes available! Insert a length of embroidery floss through the little hole in the zipper pull. Pull the tails even, and attach a pom-pom with a couple of hand stitches.

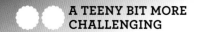
Oilcloth Tote with Fabric Handles

Whether you use it as a lunch bag or a book bag, this oilcloth tote will make you want to carry everything you can in it! It is just so darn cute!

Finished size: 7˝ × 11˝ × 4˝

> What Do I Need?

- ½ yard of oilcloth

- ½ yard of fabric for the lining

- ¼ yard of fabric for the handles

- ⅓ yard of interfacing

- 2½˝ × 2½˝ square of paper

- Large paper clips

- Basic supplies (page 12)

> Special Skills

- Refer to The Rules of Sewing (page 9)

- Using an iron (page 21)

Prepare the Pieces

1 Cut 2 pieces of oilcloth to measure 12½˝ × 15˝ each for the outside.

2 Cut 2 pieces of fabric to measure 12½˝ × 15˝ each for the lining.

3 Cut 2 pieces of fabric to measure 4˝ × 15˝ each for the handles.

4 Cut 2 pieces of interfacing to measure 4˝ × 15˝ each for the handles.

TIP

If your oilcloth fabric is a little wrinkly and crinkly, resist the urge to use an iron! Irons and oilcloth sure don't mix very well. Not only will your oilcloth be a melted mess, but your iron will be a mess too! Use a warm hairdryer held a few inches away to gently release the wrinkles. Be careful not to put it so close that the cloth starts to melt! After warming the oilcloth, I usually stack magazines on top until it has cooled.

Let's Make It!

If you are using a ¼˝ presser foot, don't forget to use washi tape as a guide to make the correct seam allowance width for this project (page 32).

THE OUTER BAG AND LINING

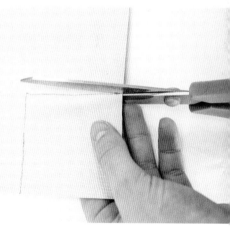

1 Line up the 2½˝ square piece of paper with the bottom corner of the oilcloth piece and trace around it with an erasable pen.

2 Do the same with the other bottom corner of the oilcloth and the other oilcloth and fabric pieces.

3 Cut out on the marked lines.

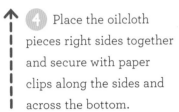

TIP

Do not use pins to hold oilcloth together. Pins will leave permanent holes. Use paper clips instead.

TIP

To make sewing on oilcloth a little easier, take the presser foot off your machine and place some masking or washi tape on the bottom of the foot. Be sure to trim off all the excess tape and use a pin to tear away the tape that is in the hole where the needle needs to go.

4 Place the oilcloth pieces right sides together and secure with paper clips along the sides and across the bottom.

5 Sew down the sides and along the bottom with the edge of the presser foot on the edge of the fabric. Make sure not to sew in the cut-out corners.

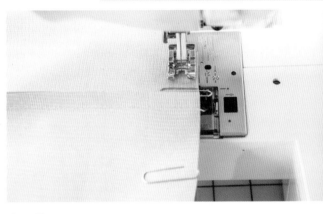

6 Bring the side and bottom seams together at both bottom cut-out corners of the bag. Place the seams so they will lie right on top of each other. The cut-out square will become a straight line with the side and bottom seams in the middle. Paper clip the raw edges together.

7 Repeat Step 6 with the other side as well and paper clip in place.

8 Sew both corners with the edge of the presser foot on the edge of the fabric.

9 Repeat these steps with the lining pieces.

Now you have an inner and an outer bag all sewn and ready to go!

THE HANDLES

① Lay the fusible interfacing on the wrong side of each of the handle pieces. Then trim all the way around to make sure there is no overhanging interfacing. Iron to fuse the interfacing in place.

② Fold the handle piece in half lengthwise with wrong sides together and press with an iron.

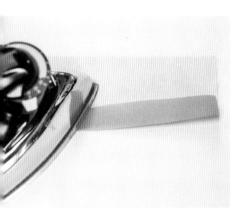

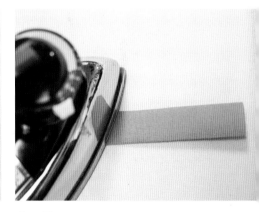

③ Open it out so you can see the center crease; then fold a side in to meet the crease and press.

④ Fold in the other side to the center crease and press.

⑤ Refold the strip on the crease so the raw edges are on the inside and press in place.

Oilcloth Tote with Fabric Handles **71**

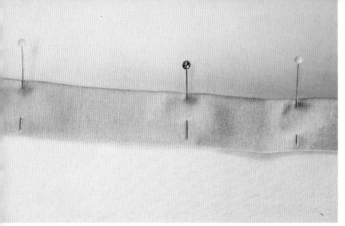

↑ ⑥ It is a good idea to use some pins to hold everything in place.

↑ ⑦ Sew nice and close to the edge down both sides of the handle.

⑧ Repeat this for the other handle.

★ TIP

It is sometimes easier to draw a sewing line with an erasable pen when you are sewing a line that is not sewn with the edge of the presser foot on the edge of the fabric.

PUT IT ALL TOGETHER

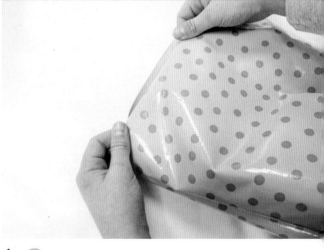

↑ ① Keep the lining piece inside out, fold over the top to the outside 1″, and press.

↑ ② Turn the oilcloth outer bag right side out and fold over the top to the inside 1″ and finger-press. Do not put the iron anywhere near the oilcloth or it will become a melted mess!

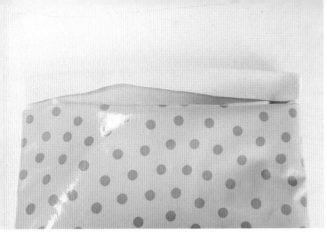

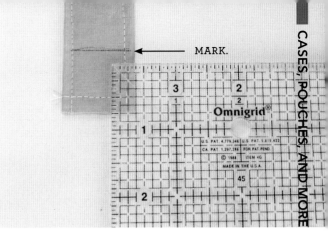

MARK.

3 Place the lining bag (inside out) in the oilcloth bag (right side out) and line up the side seams.

4 Using paper clips, clip the lining and outer bag together.

5 Mark 1″ from the ends of each of the handles.

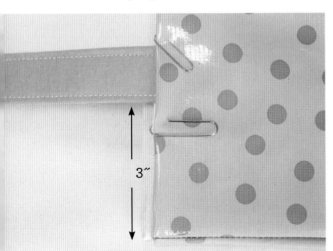

3″

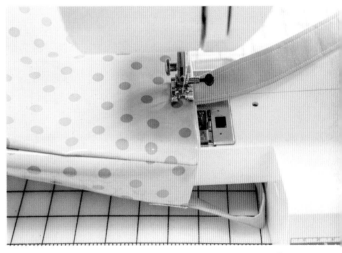

6 Measure in 3″ from the side seam of the bag and mark. Insert an end of the handle between the lining and the oilcloth at the 3″ mark and push the end in only as far as that 1″ mark. Use a paper clip to hold the handle securely in place. Repeat for the other end of the handle, placing it 3″ in from the other side seam. Do this with both handles.

7 Carefully and slowly sew around the top of the bag, removing the clips as you get to them.

8 Sew carefully over the handle area; you don't want to get the handles all caught up.

9 Trim your threads and shout "Hooray!" You are all done!

Oilcloth Tote with Fabric Handles **73**

I Heart Music MP3 Player Case

I heart music, you heart music—we all heart music. Let's all love it even more with this super-cool MP3 player case made from colorful felt!

Finished size: 3½˝ × 6˝

> What Do I Need?

- 1 piece of red felt at least 6˝ × 10˝
- 1 piece of white felt at least 3˝ × 3˝
- Double-sided fusible web at least 3˝ × 3˝
- Button
- Sewing machine
- Basic supplies (page 12)

> Special Skills

- Refer to The Rules of Sewing (page 9)
- Making and using templates (page 20)
- Using fusible web (page 22)
- Sewing on a button (page 25)
- Using an iron (page 21)
- Sewing around a corner (page 19)

Prepare the Pieces

You'll need the heart and tab patterns (page 228).

1. Cut 2 pieces of red felt 4˝ × 6˝ for the case back and front.

2. Trace the tab pattern onto parchment paper. Pin the pattern to the red felt, and cut out the tab.

3. Trace the heart pattern on the paper side of the fusible web.

4. With the paper side up, iron the fusible web heart to the white felt. Cut out the heart.

Let's Make It!

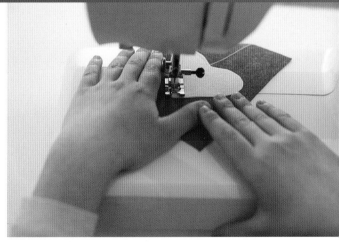

1. Peel the paper off the fusible web. Center the heart, sticky side down, on the front of a 4˝ × 6˝ felt piece. Carefully iron it on.

2. Sew around the heart. Sew slowly, close to the edge of the heart. When you get to the point of the heart, just treat it as if you were sewing around a corner. Put the needle down into the felt, lift the presser foot, and turn the felt. Put the presser foot back down, and keep on going. You can use thread in cream, white, or a pretty color.

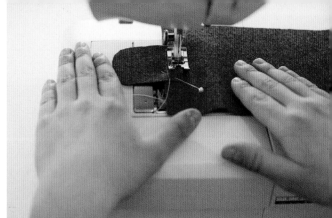

3 Now, let's attach the tab. Fold the 4˝ × 6˝ felt piece for the case back in half lengthwise to find the center. Pin the tab at this center point. Place the tab so that it is overlapping about ¼˝–½˝ on the back of the case.

4 Sew around the area where the tab overlaps the back. Sew close to the edge of the tab in a rectangular shape.

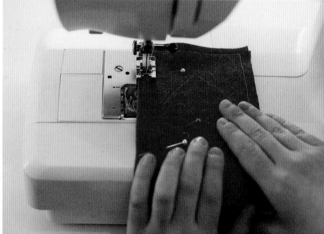

5 Lay the case front and back right sides together. Pin on 3 sides, leaving the top open.

6 Sew around the 3 sides with the edge of the presser foot on the edge of the felt. Backstitch at the beginning and end.

↑ **7** Turn the case right side out. Use the eraser end of a pencil to push out the corners.

↑ **8** Mark the spot on the case front for the button. Using button thread, hand sew it in place.

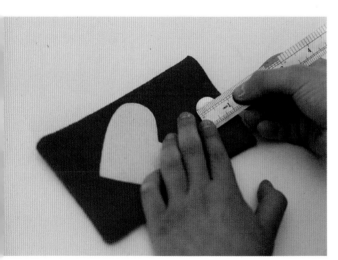

↑ **9** To make the buttonhole in the tab, first measure across the button. With sharp scissors, carefully cut the slit in the tab a little shorter than the button's width. (Felt can stretch a little!) Remember to be careful and not to cut the hole too big. You could always mark it with your disappearing-ink marker.

Pop your MP3 player in the case, and do a little dance. Hooray!

I Heart Music MP3 Player Case **77**

A TEENY BIT MORE CHALLENGING

Cross-Body Handy Pouch

You will be the coolest gal in town with this adorable bag. Add a cute apple or mushroom decoration. And go ahead—personalize it. Hang a tassel or two off the strap!

Finished size: 9½″ × 11½″

> What Do I Need?

- ½ yard of fun printed fabric for the outer bag

- ½ yard of heavier cotton for the lining

- ¼ yard of fabric for the strap

- Scraps of felt in several colors for the bag decoration (Felt scraps for the large apple and mushroom pieces need to be at least 4″ × 5″.)

- ¼ yard or large scrap of double-sided fusible web

- ⅓ yard of featherweight fusible interfacing* (I use Pellon Fusible Featherweight.)

- Sewing machine

- Basic supplies (page 12)

* Interfacing is a material that you iron onto your fabric to make it a little stiffer. Find it at fabric and quilt stores.

> Special Skills

- Refer to The Rules of Sewing (page 9)

- Making and using templates (page 20)

- Using an iron (page 21)

- Using fusible web (page 22)

- Sewing around a corner (page 19)

Prepare the Pieces

You'll need the apple and mushroom patterns (page 229).

1 Decide whether you want an apple or a mushroom for your bag decoration. Trace the pattern pieces of your choice onto the paper side of the fusible web.

2 With the paper side up, iron the fusible web pieces to the felt colors of your choice. Cut out the pieces.

TIP Make It Yours!

You can create your own design for a decoration. Draw it on the paper side of the fusible web. Then follow the directions just as for the apple or mushroom. Remember, your design will be the reverse of what you draw, so take care if you are adding a design with letters or numbers.

3 Cut 2 pieces of printed fabric 10˝ × 12˝ for the outside of the bag.

4 Cut 2 pieces of heavier fabric 10˝ × 12˝ for the lining.

5 Cut 2 pieces of featherweight fusible interfacing 10˝ × 12˝.

6 Cut 2 pieces of fabric 4˝ × 24˝ for the straps.

7 Read the package directions for the fusible interfacing. Lay 1 piece of the interfacing on the wrong side of 1 outside bag piece. The rough side of the interfacing should face the wrong side of the fabric. Iron the 2 pieces together. Make sure they are stuck nice and tight. You may need to iron back and forth a bit. Repeat with the other outside bag and interfacing pieces.

Let's Make It!

This bag has an outside, a lining, and a strap. Just work slowly and make one part at a time. Sew as slow as a snail and as straight as you can. This is really good straight-sewing practice!

OUTSIDE BAG

↑ ① Peel off the backing paper, and position your felt decoration pieces in the lower corner of the front outside bag piece.

⭐**TIP Think Ahead!**

Make sure the felt shape is not positioned too close to the edge. Otherwise, it could get caught in the seam allowance when you stitch the bag together.

Also, make sure you have the decoration exactly where you want it. Once you've ironed down the pieces, you can't move them!

↑ ② Iron down the decoration.

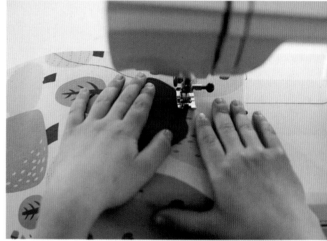

↑ ③ Sew around the edges of the felt decoration to hold it in place. Stitch nice and close to the edge of the fabric. Try your hardest to keep your stitching even.

⭐**TIP Colorful Thread**

You can use thread the same color as your decoration if you like. I personally love using black thread. It really makes the shapes stand out!

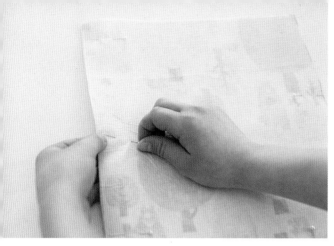

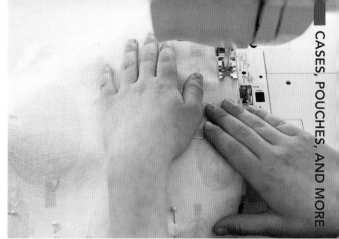

4 Let's put the bag together. Place the bag outside pieces right sides together. Pin around the sides and bottom. Leave the top open.

5 Sew the pieces together. Sew with the edge of the presser foot on the edge of the fabric. Start at the top right corner. Sew down to the bottom, across the bottom, and up the other side. Don't forget to backstitch at the beginning and end! Turn the bag right side out.

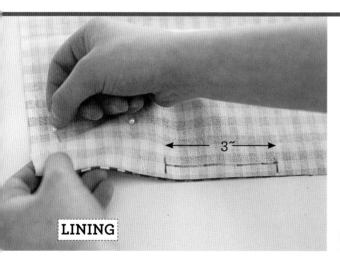

LINING

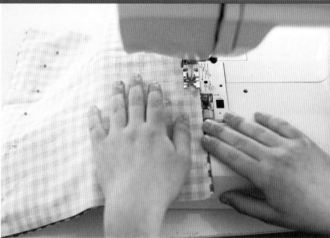

1 Place the lining front and back with right sides together. Measure a 3″ space in the center of the bottom edge. Use a disappearing-ink marker to mark a 3″ line. When you sew you will leave this 3″ unsewn so you can turn the bag right side out through the hole.

2 Sew the pieces together. Sew with the edge of the presser foot on the edge of the fabric. Start at the top right corner, and sew down to the bottom corner. Stop and turn. Sew across the bottom, but stop at the beginning of your marked 3″ line. Backstitch. Then start sewing again at the end of the marked line. Sew across the rest of the bottom and up the other side. Backstitch at every stop and start.

STRAP

1 Fold the 24″ strip in half, wrong sides together, and iron it. Now, using the center crease as a guide, fold in each long edge so they meet in the middle. Do the same with the other handle.

2 Now fold the strips in half along their length. Iron them nice and flat.

3 Topstitch down both edges of each strap. Sew nice and close to the edge.

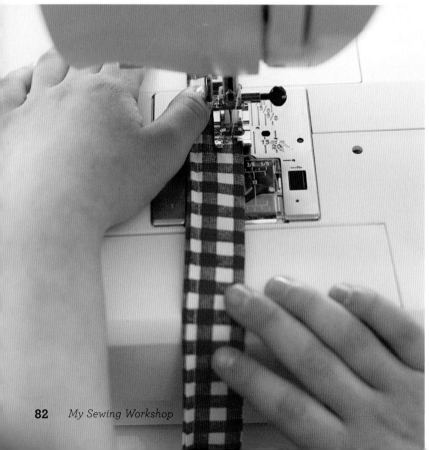

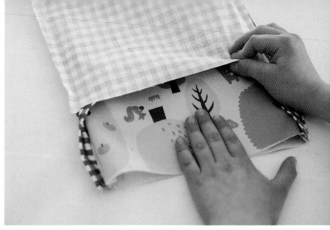

PUT IT TOGETHER

1 Pin one end of each strap to the outside bag, centered on a side seam of the bag. (Look carefully at the picture.) Line up the ends with the bag top, and pin.

2 With the lining still inside out, gently push the outside bag into the lining. Keep the strap facing down toward the bottom, out of the way. Line up the tops of the inside and outside bags. Pin all the way around. Before you start sewing, make sure that the straps are pushed down into the bag and not all bunched up in there.

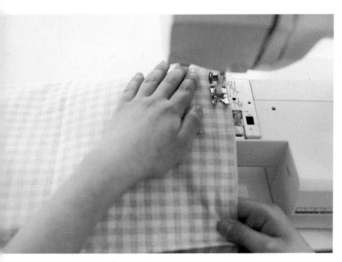

3 You may need to take the extension table off your machine if you have one. This makes it easier to sew around the top in a kind of circle. Sew all the way around with the edge of the presser foot on the edge of the fabric, and remove the pins.

4 Remember the 3˝ gap you left in the lining bottom? Carefully pull the bag right side out through that hole.

↑ **5** Fold in the edges of the hole you left in the lining piece. Iron. Topstitch the hole closed. Sew close to the edge!

↑ **6** Push the lining down into the bag. Make sure to push out the corners well.

↑ **7** Yay! Now you just need to iron around the top.

↑ **8** Now tie the handle ends together in a knot. You can tie the knot high or low. It all depends on how long or short you want your bag handles to be!

Cross-Body Handy Pouch **85**

Super-Sweet-Smelling Lavender Sachets

There is something about the smell of lavender that makes me feel happy. Now it's time to spread the happiness and make these sweet-smelling lavender sachets for all your friends. Pop one in your pillow for sweet dreams or stash it in your drawer to keep your clothes smelling fresh ... Mmmmmm.

Finished size:
Approximately 4¾˝ × 6½˝

❯ What Do I Need?

- Large scrap at least 6˝ × 15˝ or ¼ yard of cotton fabric for the outer bag (You can make 3 bags with ¼ yard.)

- Large scrap at least 5˝ × 14˝ of muslin for the inner bag

- ⅛ yard of fun-colored cotton for the ties

- Dried lavender (about 1 cup)

- Basic supplies (page 12)

❯ Special Skills

- Refer to The Rules of Sewing (page 9)

- Using an iron (page 21)

¦ Prepare the Pieces

1 Cut 1 piece of cotton fabric to measure 5½″ × 14″ for the outer bag.

2 Cut 1 piece of muslin to measure 4½″ × 13″ for the inner bag.

3 Cut 2 pieces of cotton to measure 2″ × 22½″ for the ties.

¦ Let's Make It!

If you are using a ¼″ presser foot, don't forget to use washi tape as a guide to make the correct seam allowance width for this project (page 32).

THE INNER BAG

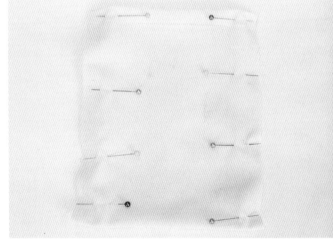

1 Fold both short ends of the piece of muslin in ½″ and press with an iron.

2 Fold the piece of fabric in half crosswise and pin down both sides, making sure to keep the folded ends on the outside.

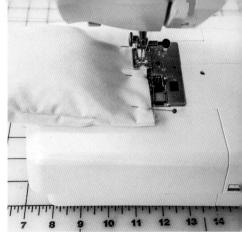

③ Sew down both sides with the edge of the presser foot on the edge of the fabric.

④ Turn the muslin lining right side out and fill with lavender. Make sure you do not overfill the bag.

⑤ Pin the opening closed.

⑥ Sew along the edge of the bag nice and close to the edge.

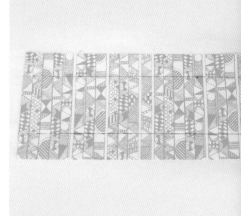

THE OUTER BAG

① Fold in both short ends of the main fabric piece ¼˝, then fold ¼˝ again, and press with an iron.

② Stitch down the fold nice and close to the edge.

③ With the right side of the fabric facing up, use an erasable pen to mark 1¼˝ in from each long side of the fabric piece.

THE TIES

↑ **1** Fold the piece of tie fabric in half lengthwise, wrong sides together, and press with an iron.

↑ **2** Open out the fabric strip and fold in each end ¼˝ and press. Next fold in a side to meet the center crease and press with an iron.

↑ **3** Fold in the other side to meet the center crease and press with an iron.

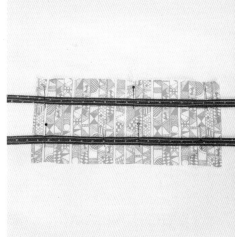

↑ **4** Refold the strip on the crease so the raw edges are on the inside and press with an iron.

↑ **5** Sew the ties around all 4 sides nice and close to the edge.

↑ **6** Place a tie along the inner side of the marks on the fabric piece. Make sure that roughly the same length of the tie extends beyond the fabric at both ends. Repeat with the other tie, placing it along the other mark.

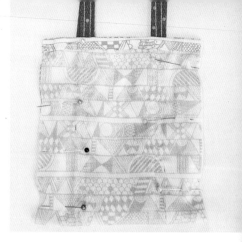

↑ ⑦ Pin the ties in place.

↑ ⑧ Sew on top of the previous stitch lines down both sides, backstitching at the beginning and end.

↑ ⑨ Fold the outer bag piece in half with right sides together and pin down both sides.

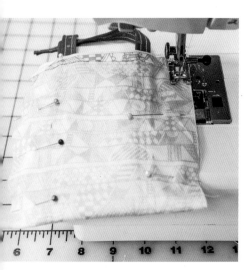
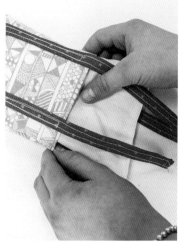
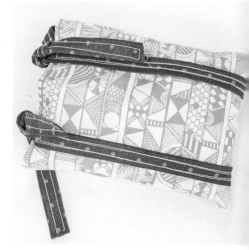

↑ ⑩ Sew down both sides with the edge of the foot on the edge of the fabric.

↑ ⑪ Turn the bag right side out.

↑ ⑫ Place the lavender sachet inside the bag and tie the ties neatly.

Make a whole stack for all your friends!

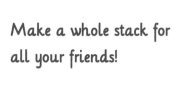

**TAKE YOUR TIME
AND ASK FOR HELP**

Super-Cute Gadget Case

Whether it's for a tablet or an e-reader or even just used as a sweet little purse, everyone will love this cute and handy bag!

Finished size:
Approximately 9¼˝ × 12¼˝

› What Do I Need?

- Fat quarter of quilting fabric for the outer case (see Fat Quarter, page 31)

- Fat quarter of cotton fabric for the lining

- ⅛ yard of fabric for the handle

- 15˝ × 24˝ of cotton quilt batting

- 10˝ of colored ribbon or elastic (½˝–1˝ wide)

- 2 metal clasps called trigger snap hooks (These can be found in a hardware store.)

- Button, ⅝˝–¾˝ size (You may want to wait to choose the button until after sewing the bag to be sure you have a button that will fit in the loop.)

- Basic supplies (page 12)

› Special Skills

- Refer to The Rules of Sewing (page 9)

- Using an iron (page 21)

- Sewing on a button (page 25)

- Sewing around a corner (page 19)

★ TIP

Look for a quilting fabric with a geometric design or even a fun plaid or check. You will be stitching on the fabric, and it looks super cute if you have a bold pattern to follow.

Prepare the Pieces

1. Cut 2 pieces of outer fabric to measure 10˝ × 13˝ each.

2. Cut 2 pieces of batting to measure 12˝ × 15˝ each.

3. Cut 2 pieces of lining fabric to measure 10˝ × 13˝ each.

4. Cut 1 piece of handle fabric to measure 2˝ × 40˝.

5. Cut 3 pieces of colored ribbon or elastic to measure 3˝ each for the handles and closure.

★ TIP

Cut the outer fabric and lining fabric as shown. It will not fit if the pieces face in the other direction.

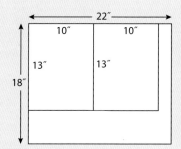

Let's Make It!

If you are using a ¼˝ presser foot, don't forget to use washi tape as a guide to make the correct seam allowance width for this project (page 32).

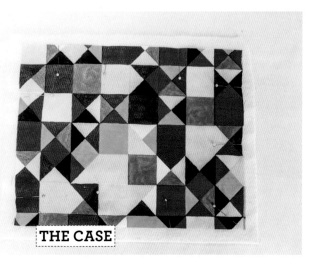

THE CASE

1. Lay the outer fabric on top of the batting piece and pin in place.

2. Machine stitch over lines in the print of the fabric or use an erasable marker to draw your own simple geometric design or simple lines. It's up to you!

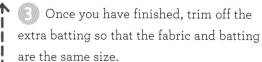

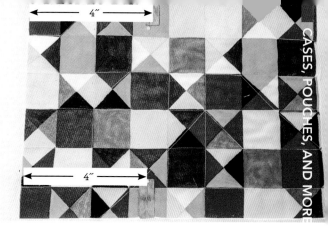

↑ ③ Once you have finished, trim off the extra batting so that the fabric and batting are the same size.

↑ ④ Repeat Steps 1–3 with the other piece of fabric and batting.

↑ ⑤ Fold 2 of the 3″ ribbon or elastic pieces in half crosswise. Measure 4″ up from the bottom of both sides of the outer bag fabric and pin a folded ribbon so that the raw edges are lined up and the fold faces toward the middle of the bag. It may seem strange to put it in this way, but I promise it will all make sense in the end. Be sure to put the pins perpendicular to the edge so you can easily remove them later. Repeat on the other side of the bag.

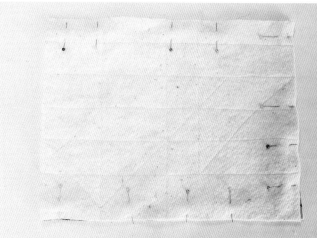

↑ ⑥ Place the outer fabric pieces right sides together.

↑ ⑦ Pin them together around 3 sides; leave a short end open.

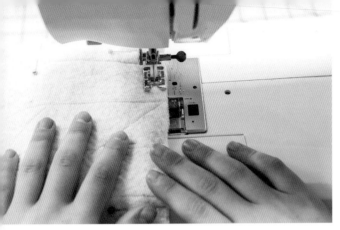

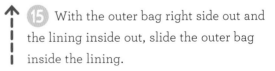

↑ **8** Sew around the 3 sides with the edge of the presser foot on the edge of the fabric. The ribbon will be sewn in this seam.

9 Turn the outer bag right side out and press with an iron.

↑ **10** Pin the lining pieces right sides together, leaving the top open.

11 Mark a 4″ no-sew zone in the bottom for turning.

↑ **12** Sew around the 3 sides, but don't forget the no-sew zone!

13 Measure exactly halfway across the top opening of the outer bag and mark the halfway point.

14 Pin a folded piece of ribbon or elastic to the marked spot. Make sure the loop is facing down with the raw edges lined up.

↑ **15** With the outer bag right side out and the lining inside out, slide the outer bag inside the lining.

94

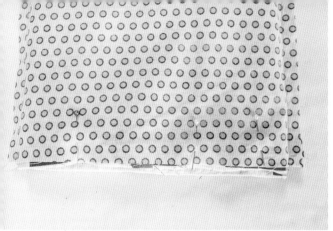

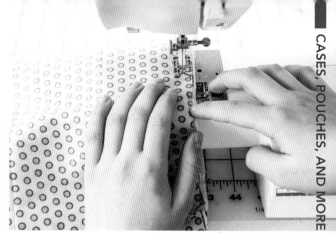

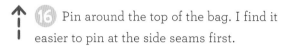

16 Pin around the top of the bag. I find it easier to pin at the side seams first.

17 If you have an open-arm sewing machine, pull the extension table off your machine and slide the top of the bag on the machine. You will be sewing around in a circle. Start sewing around the top with the edge of the presser foot on the edge of the fabric. Stop when you get around to where you started.

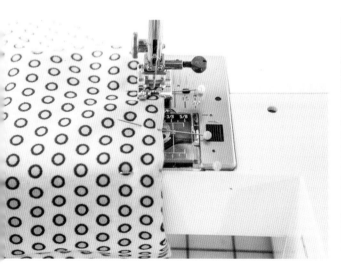

THE HANDLE

18 Pull the bag right side out through the hole at the bottom of the lining.

19 Pin the hole closed and sew close to the edge.

20 Push the lining inside the bag, making sure to push out all the corners.

1 Fold the handle fabric strip in half lengthwise with wrong sides together. Press with an iron.

↑ **2** Open out the strip so you can see the crease and fold in each long edge to meet the center crease. Press with an iron.

↑ **3** Refold the strip on the center crease so the raw edges are on the inside and press really well with an iron.

↑ **4** Use pins to hold the strip together while you are sewing.

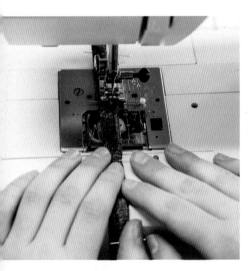
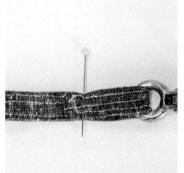

Finish Up!

↑ **5** Sew down both sides nice and close to the edge of the fabric.

↑ **6** Loop an end of the handle through the loop on the clasp and pull it through about 1″. Sew the handle in place, being sure to backstitch a few times to make it extra secure. Repeat with the other end of the handle.

7 Clip the clasps to the elastic or ribbon loops.

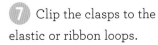

↑ Fold the bag top over and mark the spot for the button. Choose a button that will comfortably fit through the elastic or ribbon loop and sew the button in place. How do I sew a button? Go to Sewing on a Button (page 25) to find out!

EASY PEASY

Sewn Gift Bags

With these fun fabric gift bags, wrapping your gift can be almost as much fun as making it. They have a great dual purpose of holding your gift and then being a useful little bag for storing special things!

Finished size:
Approximately 7¾˝ × 9⅝˝

> What Do I Need?

- Fat quarter of fun fabric (see Fat Quarter, page 31)

- Approximately 24˝ of fun-colored twine

- Basic supplies (page 12)

> Special Skills

- Refer to The Rules of Sewing (page 9)

- Using an iron (page 21)

- Sewing around a corner (page 19)

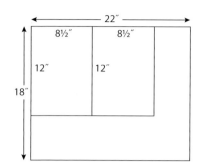

Prepare the Pieces

Cut 2 pieces of fabric 8½″ × 12″ using the diagram as your guide.

Let's Make It!

If you are using a ¼″ presser foot, don't forget to use washi tape as a guide to make the correct seam allowance width for this project (page 32).

1 Place the 2 fabric pieces right sides together and pin down a long (12″) side.

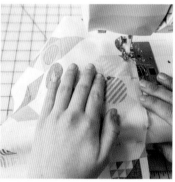

2 Sew down that side with the edge of the presser foot on the edge of the fabric.

3 Open out the seam and iron it flat.

4 Fold in ½″ on each of the remaining 12″-long sides and press with an iron.

5 Fold down the top 1½″ and press with an iron.

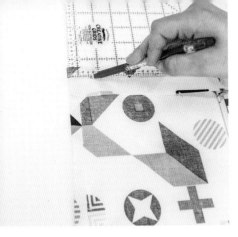

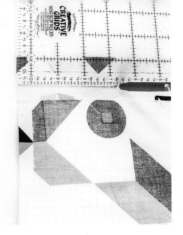

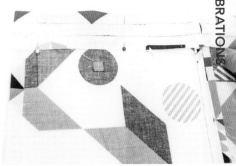

6 Use an erasable-ink pen to draw a line ½˝ from the top folded edge. Extend the line to go from side to side across the entire top.

7 Draw another line ½˝ under the first line.

8 Pin the top folded edge down to hold it in place while you sew.

9 Sew on both lines, making sure to backstitch at the beginning and end.

10 Fold the piece in half with right sides together and pin. Placing the edge of the presser foot at the edge of the fabric and starting just under the second line of stitching, stitch down the side edge and across the bottom of the bag. Backstitch at the beginning and end.

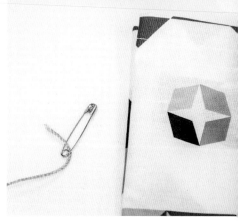

↑ ⑪ Trim the corners—but don't cut the stitching!

↑ ⑫ Turn the bag right side out and press with an iron.

↑ ⑬ Attach a small safety pin to the end of a length of twine at least 24˝ long.

↑ ⑭ Feed the safety pin through the little casing you created with the 2 lines of stitching. Go all the way through the casing and bring the pin out through the opening on the other side.

↑ ⑮ Decide on the length of twine you want the finished bag to have and cut the ends even. Tie the ends together with a knot.

Once you know how to make this fun bag, start experimenting with different sizes. You could make a big wide one or maybe a tall skinny one .. it's up to you!

Attach a sweet card and maybe a pom-pom or two and you are set!

Paper Flower Gift Toppers

Add a little taste of spring to your gift with this super-sweet paper flower gift topper. When the gift is opened, the flower could be sewn to a hair clip and worn in the recipient's hair ... how lovely!

Finished size:
Approximately 7″ in diameter

> What Do I Need?

- Crepe paper in colors that would make a fun flower
- Scrap of felt measuring at least 3″ × 3″ for the flower base
- Hot glue gun (low temperature)
- Paper scissors

> Special Skills

- Refer to The Rules of Sewing (page 9)
- Making and using templates (page 20)
- Using a hot glue gun (page 23)

Prepare the Pieces

You'll need the paper flower topper pattern pieces (pages 229 and 230).

1 Use the patterns to make templates.

2 Cut a stack of 6-8 of each different-sized petal from crepe paper.

3 Cut 1 strip for the inside of the flower from crepe paper.

4 Cut 1 felt circle.

> ★ **TIP**
> *Always cut the petals so that the grain (the lines in the crepe paper) is running up and down. This helps when it comes to shaping the petals.*

Let's Make It!

1 Use your fingers to gently shape and stretch the petals so that they look a bit more like real flower petals.

2 Starting around the outside edge of the felt circle, glue a couple of rows of overlapping large petals.

  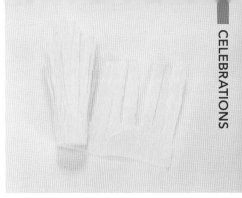

3 Gradually start building the flower by adding rows of medium-sized petals inside the large petals.

4 Next, fill in by adding rows of small petals.

5 To make the inside of the flower, cut a fringe edge on the crepe paper strip.

6 Roll up the fringe and secure with a bit of hot glue.

7 Attach it to the center of the flower.

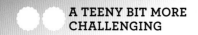
Hoop Treats

What could be cuter than a little framed mushroom or cupcake? These projects are a great way to use little scraps of your favorite fabrics. Better watch out—you won't be able to stop at just one!

Finished size: 6˝

> What Do I Need?

Makes 1 hoop treat.

- 1 piece of cotton canvas fabric measuring at least 8˝ × 8˝
- Small scraps of 3 different fabrics for the design
- Double-sided fusible web
- Little piece of ribbon
- 6˝ wooden embroidery hoop (Find it at a fabric or craft store.)
- Sewing machine
- Basic supplies (page 12)

> Special Skills

- Refer to The Rules of Sewing (page 9)
- Making and using templates (page 20)
- Using fusible web (page 22)
- Using an iron (page 21)

Prepare the Pieces

You'll need the cupcake and mushroom patterns (page 230).

1 Trace your chosen pattern pieces onto the paper side of the fusible web. (The mushroom and cupcake each have 3 pieces.)

2 Follow the directions on the package to iron the fusible web (with the rough side of the web down) onto your fabrics.

3 Cut out the pieces.

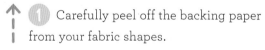

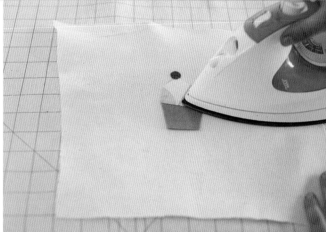

1 Carefully peel off the backing paper from your fabric shapes.

2 Position them on the canvas fabric, sticky side down. Try to center the design, but if you're off a little, that's okay. Iron the pieces in place.

3 Thread your machine needle and bobbin with black thread. Sew close to the edge around your design. It doesn't have to look perfect. If you want to, stitch some up-and-down lines on the cupcake "paper." Look at the pictures for a guide.

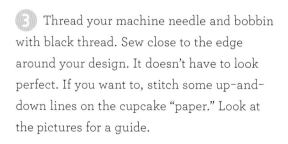

↑ **4** Take apart the wooden hoop, and lay the inner piece on a table. Center the canvas on top. Loosen the outer hoop screw (not too loose). Gently push it onto the canvas and inner hoop with the hoop's screw at the top.

↑ **5** Pull gently on the fabric to keep it taut and wrinkle free. Tighten the screw to hold everything in place.

↑ **6** Check that it all looks good. Then carefully trim off the excess fabric around the back of the hoop.

↑ **7** Tie on a ribbon, and hang it on your wall!

What other things could you find to use as a frame? Start thinking creatively!

EASY PEASY

Super Quick Bunting

This super quick fabric bunting is so fun to make, you will be stringing it all over the place.

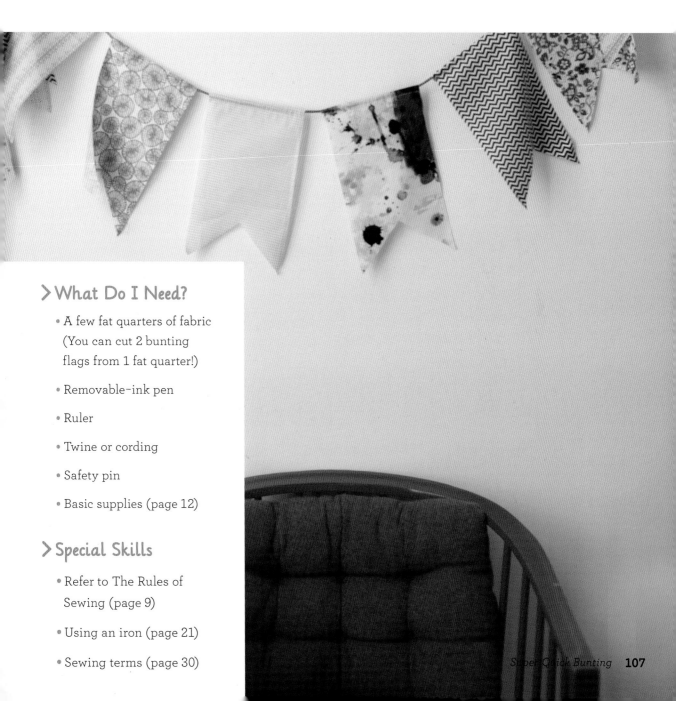

> What Do I Need?

- A few fat quarters of fabric (You can cut 2 bunting flags from 1 fat quarter!)
- Removable-ink pen
- Ruler
- Twine or cording
- Safety pin
- Basic supplies (page 12)

> Special Skills

- Refer to The Rules of Sewing (page 9)
- Using an iron (page 21)
- Sewing terms (page 30)

Prepare the Pieces

1 Cut a little pile of flag pieces, each measuring 8½″ × 12″.

You can make as many as you like. It all depends on how long you want the bunting to be.

2 Using the removable-ink pen, mark a 3″-long vertical line centered along the bottom short edge of the flag.

- - - - - - - - - - - - - - - - - →

↑ **3** Draw a line from the top of the center line to the lower left-hand corner of the flag.

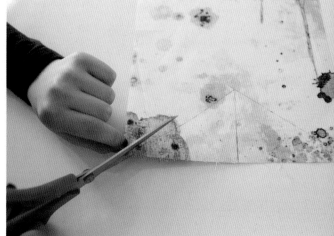

↑ **4** Do the same with the lower right-hand corner.

5 Remove the drawn triangle shape by cutting along the diagonal lines.

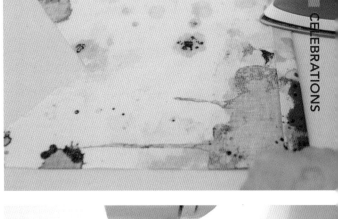

¡ Let's Make It!

1 Fold the top edge of the flag over ½˝ to the wrong side, and iron.

2 Fold over ½˝ again, and iron.

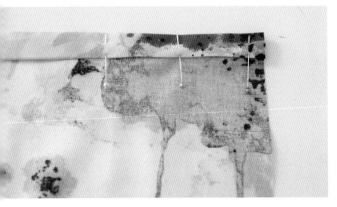

↑ **3** Pin down the fold.

↑ **4** Sew nice and close to the first folded edge.

Do this for all your flags.

¡ Finish Up!

↑ **1** Lay all the flags out in a line, and arrange the fabrics in a way that you like.

String it up inside or outside for an instant party!

↑ **2** Cut a piece of twine or cording at least 20˝ longer than the total width of all the flags.

3 Attach a safety pin to the end of the twine or cording, and thread through all the flags.

Yo-Yo Garland

Every day will be a celebration with this cute-as-a-button yo-yo garland. You will love making these fun yo-yo circles and sewing them into a fun strand to use for a party or give as the sweetest handmade gift ever!

>What Do I Need?

- Fabric scraps slightly larger than the pattern pieces (approximately 8˝ × 8˝ for the large yo-yo and 6˝ × 6˝ for the small yo-yo)

- Basic supplies (page 12)

>Special Skills

- Refer to The Rules of Sewing (page 9)

- Making and using templates (page 20)

- Sewing a running stitch (page 26)

- Sewing a whipstitch (page 28)

★ TIP

I have included patterns for 2 different sizes of yo-yo circles just in case you want to vary the design of the garland a little. The large finished yo-yo is approximately 3¼˝ in diameter, and the small finished yo-yo is approximately 2¼˝ in diameter.

Prepare the Pieces

You'll need the large and small yo-yo patterns (page 231).

Trace the large and small yo-yo patterns on paper and cut out. Use the patterns to cut a few circles out of fabric in varying sizes.

Let's Make It!

1. Thread an arm's length of button thread into the needle and knot the end about 2˝ from the end.

Note *An arm's length of thread is measured from your fingertips to your shoulder. This makes the thread piece a little easier to manage.*

2. Fold over the outer edges of the circle approximately ¼˝ and use your finger to press a little crease. We will be folding the edge over as we go along. You may want to pin the fold down as you go; it is up to you.

3. Find the center-ish of the folded seam allowance and bring the needle through the fabric from the front of the yo-yo to the back. We will be working with the yo-yo wrong side up.

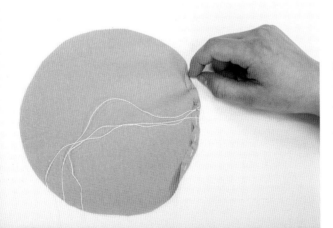

4. Start sewing a long ½˝ running stitch all the way around the circle, trying hard to keep your stitching in the center of the fold.

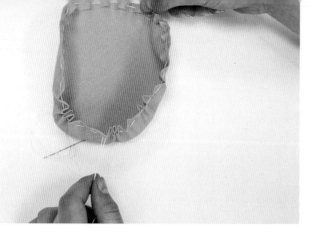

5 When you get to the end, carefully pull both ends of the button thread to gather the circle in the middle, flattening and evening the gathering as you go along. Keep pulling and adjusting the gathers until you are happy with how it looks.

6 Tie the thread tail to the other end of the thread, knot 4 times, and trim your threads. Smooth out the yo-yo with your hands just to get things nice and flat.

7 Make as many yo-yos as you need for your cute garland. Make it as short or as long as you want!

¡Finish Up!

1 Arrange the yo-yos in the order you like.

2 Use an erasable pen to mark the joining spots on each yo-yo.

3 Thread your needle with button thread and use a whipstitch to sew each yo-yo to its neighbor. Just a couple of stitches should do it, and be sure to knot everything off when you are done!

String up your garland and enjoy all that gorgeousness!

EASY PEASY

Fabric Tassel Garland

Every day is a crafty celebration with these fun fabric tassels. Choose some cheery fabric, and start cutting.

❯ What Do I Need?

- A selection of fat quarters of fabric
- Ruler
- Sharp scissors
- Twine
- Cording

¡ Let's Make It!

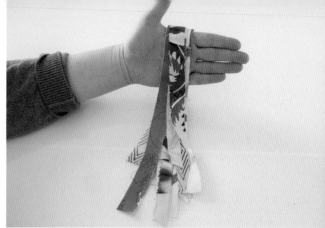

1 Using a variety of different fabrics, cut a pile of strips measuring 20˝ long and around ¾˝–1˝ wide. You'll need 90 or more strips.

✦TIP

They don't all have to be perfect, so don't worry too much!

2 Cut 10 lengths of twine, each 5˝.

3 Each tassel will have 9 fabric strips. Start by laying your fabric strips across your hand, adding them one by one with the print facing up.

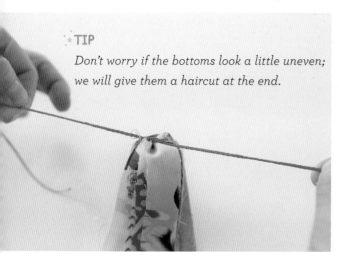

✦TIP

Don't worry if the bottoms look a little uneven; we will give them a haircut at the end.

4 Gather them in the center, and tie them tightly with a piece of twine.

5 Repeat this process for all the other strips until you have 10 (or as many as you want) fabric tassels.

6 Now give them a little trim so they are all the same length.

7 Tie them to a long piece of cording at even intervals. Cut off the excess twine from the tassels.

Hang your awesome garland somewhere fabulous!

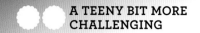

Happiness Storage Trays

These cute-as-a-button little trays are perfect for storing all your little treasures. Make a few to hold your favorite collections!

Finished size: 6˝ × 6˝

> What Do I Need?

- Piece of quilting-weight cotton print fabric at least 10˝ × 10˝ for the inside of the tray

- Piece of heavyweight cotton print fabric at least 10˝ × 10˝ for the outside of the tray*

- Piece of cotton batting at least 10˝ × 10˝

- 8 assorted fun flat buttons (with holes)

- Sewing machine

- Basic supplies (page 12)

* The heavier fabric on the outside helps make the tray nice and stiff.

> Special Skills

- Refer to The Rules of Sewing (page 9)

- Sewing on a button (page 25)

- Using an iron (page 21)

- Sewing around a corner (page 19)

- Topstitch (page 33)

Prepare the Pieces

1 Cut a 9″ × 9″ square from each of the 2 fabrics. Cut 1 from the batting, too.

2 Make a sandwich with the squares. Lay the batting on the bottom. Put the outside fabric square over it, right side facing up. Then put the inside fabric on top, with the right side down.

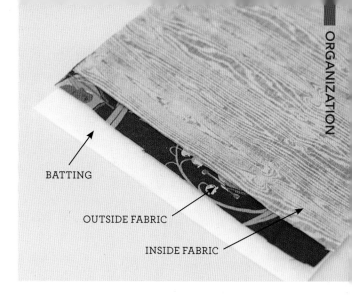

BATTING

OUTSIDE FABRIC

INSIDE FABRIC

Let's Make It!

1 Make sure the pieces are lined up square. Pin around all 4 sides.

2 Use the disappearing-ink marker to draw a 3″ line centered along one edge.

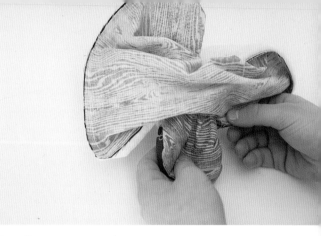

↑ ③ Sew the pieces together. Sew with the edge of the presser foot on the edge of the fabric. Start at the top corner. Sew down to the bottom corner, and turn. Sew across the bottom to the beginning of the marked line. Start stitching again at the other end of the line; sew up the other side and around to the starting corner. Don't forget to backstitch at each start and stop!

↑ ④ Sometimes the corners can seem a little bulky, so you may want to trim the corners. Do not cut into the stitching! Turn your tray right side out. The batting should be on the inside of the tray!

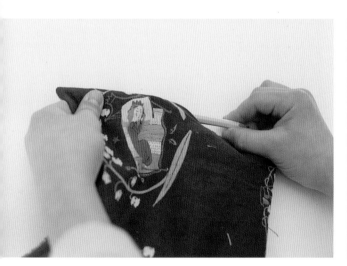

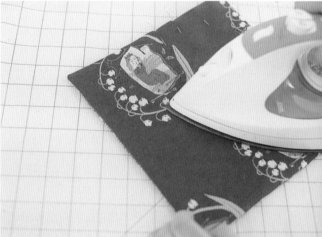

↑ ⑤ Use the eraser end of a pencil to push out the corners so they are nice and neat.

↑ ⑥ Time to turn on the iron. Carefully fold in the edges that are still open. Pin them in place. Iron the entire tray so it looks super neat and flat.

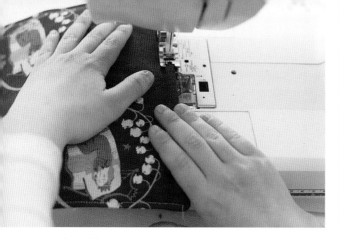

↑ ⑦ Topstitch ¼˝ from the edge all the way around the square. This will make the edge look neat. It also closes up the opening in the edge of the square.

↑ ⑧ Mark a 6˝ × 6˝ square exactly in the center of the square you have just sewn. Use your disappearing-ink marker. Hint: You can use a 6˝ square ruler as shown here. Or just measure with a regular ruler. Ask an adult for help.

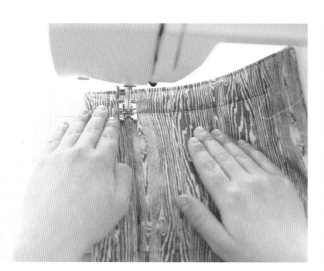

↑ ⑨ Before the disappearing ink actually disappears, sew around the square that you just marked.

↑ ⑩ Using your disappearing-ink marker and a ruler, draw a line from a corner of the inner stitching to the corner of the square. This will be your guide for folding the corner. Repeat in the other 3 corners.

↑ ⑪ Make a fold at a corner. (Look closely at the photo.) Make sure the top edges of the tray look even. Pin to hold the fold in place. Do this with all the corners.

↑ ⑫ Imagine a line going from the bottom corner of the tray straight up. Find the halfway point, and mark it with a dot. This will be the button spot.

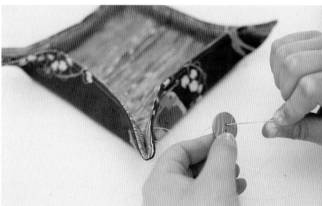

↑ ⑬ Use button thread in your needle. Push the needle and thread through one side of the folded corner, and then push it back through to the first side. Leave a nice long tail. Tie the tail and needle thread together with a knot. Be sure to pull tight to hold the corner together.

↑ ⑮ Now add another button to the other side of the corner. Go up through the first hole and then down through the remaining hole on that button and carefully back through to the side you started from.

⑭ Now push your needle through the hole of 1 button, and sew back through the second hole to the other side of the corner.

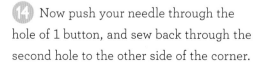

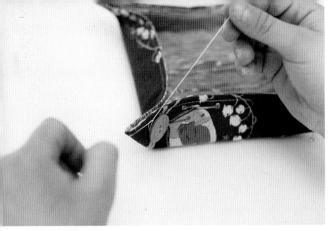

16 Tie a knot using the thread and the tail you left from the knot. Make sure to tie the knot behind the button and trim the thread so it doesn't show. It sounds complicated, but it really isn't! Be careful not to prick your fingers! Now do this with the remaining corners.

Yippee-ki-yay ... you did it! Don't you just love your super-cute tray?

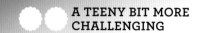
Scrappy Patchy Pencil Cup

Everyone needs somewhere to put stray pens and pencils. What's better than this super-cool patchy pencil cup? Maybe they will make you want to spend more time writing ...

❯ What Do I Need?

- Scraps at least 7˝ long of fun fabric

- Mason jar (We used a jar measuring 6½˝ tall, but you can use any size for this project.)

- ¼ yard of plain canvas fabric for the backing

- Fun-colored sewing machine thread

- Basic supplies (page 12)

❯ Special Skills

- Refer to The Rules of Sewing (page 9)

- Using an iron (page 21)

Prepare the Pieces

1 Use a tape measure to measure the jar from the base to just under the lid area. Now add ½″ and write that measurement down. It will be the height of your cover. (My jar measures 5½″, with the addition of ½″ to make a measurement of 6″.)

2 Measure around the circumference of the jar. Add ¾″ and write down the measurement. (Mine is 12¼″, with the addition of ¾″ to make a measurement of 13″.)

3 Cut the canvas the height and width of the measurements that you wrote down in Steps 1 and 2. (In my case, 6″ × 13″.)

4 Cut a variety of fabric scraps a bit longer than the height (in my case, approximately 6½″) and to whatever width you like.

Let's Make It!

If you are using a ¼″ presser foot, don't forget to use washi tape as a guide to make the correct seam allowance width for this project (page 32).

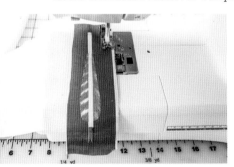

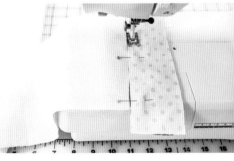

1 Start by placing the first fabric right side up along an end of the canvas and pin. Stitch it down close to the long fabric edge at the end of the canvas.

2 Lay the second strip right side down on top of the first strip, so that the long edges are lined up; pin.

3 Sew with the edge of the presser foot on the long edge of the fabric strip.

Scrappy Patchy Pencil Cup **123**

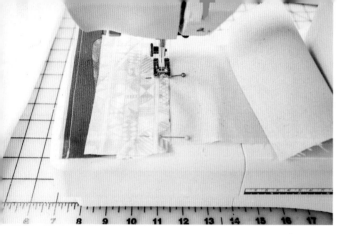

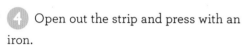

↑ 4 Open out the strip and press with an iron.

5 Lay the third strip right side down on the second strip and sew in the same way. Open out to press. Continue until the entire canvas piece is covered with fabric strips.

↑ 6 Iron the entire piece well.

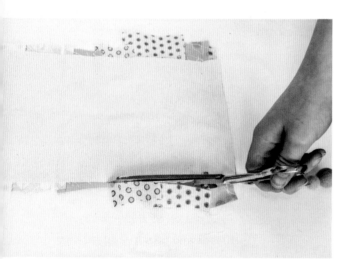

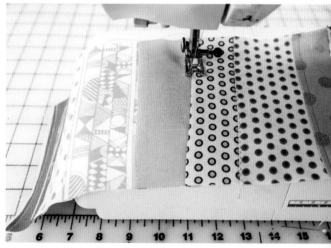

↑ 7 Secure the last strip by sewing down close to the outer edge.

8 Turn the piece over and trim it even with the canvas edges.

↑ 9 Time to do some fun stitching! Take this moment to explore some other stitches on your machine and get creative stitching over seams.

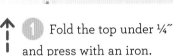

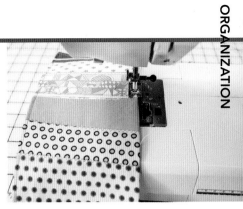

↑ 1 Fold the top under ¼˝ and press with an iron.

↑ 2 Sew close to the edge.

↑ 3 Fold the bottom under ¼˝. Press with an iron and sew close to the edge.

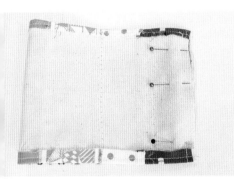

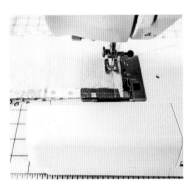

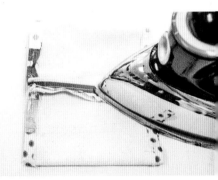

↑ 4 Fold the finished piece in half, right sides facing, and pin the ends together.

↑ 5 Sew with the edge of the foot on the edge of the fabric.

↑ 6 Press the seam open with an iron.

7 Trim off all those pesky threads and turn it right side out.

8 Slide the sleeve onto the mason jar.

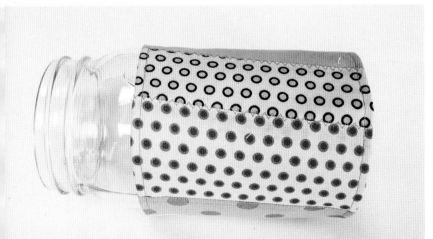

← – – – – – – – – – – – – –

What a great transformation!

Super-Secret Journal Cover

We all need somewhere to keep our secrets. Now you can keep yours in a notebook with your very own handmade cover. Keep it secure with a ribbon that you wrap and tie around it.

Finished size: 15˝ × 10˝

> What Do I Need?

- ½ yard of printed cotton fabric for the outside cover
- ½ yard of fabric for the inside cover
- 1 yard of ½˝-wide ribbon
- 4 felt scraps each at least 2˝ × 2˝ for the flowers
- Small pom-poms (Find them at a craft supply store.)
- Marble composition book, 7½˝ × 9¾˝*
- Sewing machine
- Basic supplies (page 12)

* These are the black notebooks with ruled pages that you can find in any office supply store.

> Special Skills

- Refer to The Rules of Sewing (page 9)
- Making and using templates (page 20)
- Using an iron (page 21)
- Using a hot glue gun (page 23)
- Sewing around a corner (page 19)

Prepare the Pieces

You'll need the flower pattern (page 231).

1. Cut 2 pieces of print fabric 11½˝ × 26¼˝. These will be the front and inside cover.

2. Trace the flower pattern, and cut 4 flowers out of felt.

Let's Make It!

 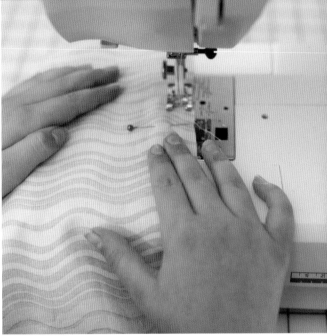

1. Place the front and inside pieces right sides together. Pin all the way around. Measure 3˝ along the bottom edge. Use the disappearing-ink marker to mark a 3˝ line. You will leave this 3˝ unsewn so you can turn the cover right side out through the hole.

2. With the edge of the presser foot on the edge of the fabric, sew all the way around the rectangle. Sew as straight as you can! Stitch from the top of the right side around the corner to the beginning of your 3˝ mark. Backstitch. Start stitching again at the end of the marked line. Stitch back to where you began. Remember to backstitch each time you start and stop.

↑ ③ Cut the points off all 4 corners. Don't cut your stitching!

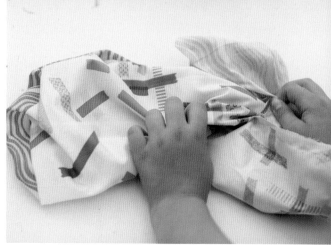

↑ ④ Turn the cover right side out, and iron it. Be sure to fold in the open edge, and iron it neatly.

↑ ⑤ Time to sew it closed. Make sure to sew nice and close to the edge.

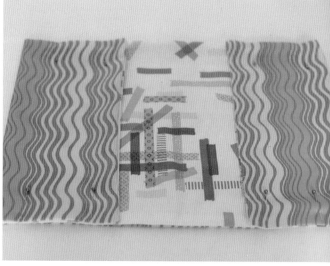

↑ ⑥ With outside fabrics facing, fold in one side of the piece of fabric 5″, and iron it in place. Repeat this with the other side. This will create the inside flaps. Now pin both flaps in place.

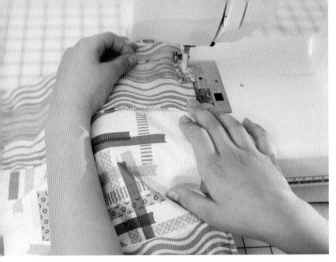

↑ (7) Sew close to the edges on each folded end. You will need to sew about ⅛˝ from the edge of the fabric. Sew nice and straight! Repeat this with the other end.

↑ (8) Turn the book cover ends right side out. Use a chopstick to push out the corners.

(9) Give your cover a good iron to make it nice and flat.

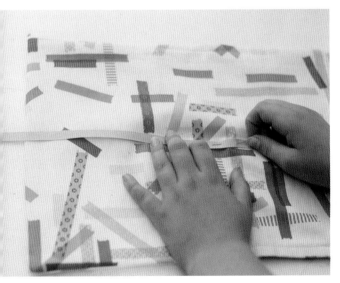

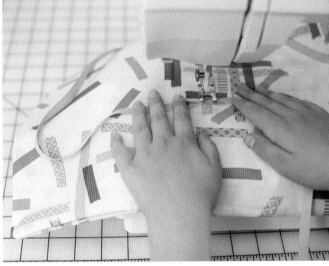

↑ (10) Fold the piece of ribbon in half to find the middle. Do the same with the cover. Pin the ribbon to the center of the outside of the cover.

↑ (11) Sew on the ribbon at this center point. Sew it in place securely.

↑ ⑫ Put a dab of hot glue on 2 felt flowers. Sandwich them together with a ribbon end in between. Repeat with the 2 other flowers and the other ribbon end.

↑ ⑬ Carefully hot glue the small pom-poms to each side of the flowers.

Now put the cover on your book, and start writing your secrets! Just remember to hide it away somewhere safe!

EASY PEASY

Bed Book Storage

Who knew that making a place to stash your books would be so easy?
This fun project will have you channeling your inner bookworm in no time!

> What Do I Need?

- ½ yard of upholstery-weight fabric, at least 54˝ wide

- 1 fat quarter of fun coordinating fabric

- Removable-ink pen

- Basic supplies (page 12)

> Special Skills

- Refer to The Rules of Sewing (page 9)

- Using an iron (page 21)

- Sewing terms (page 30)

¡ Prepare the Pieces

1 Cut 2 pieces of upholstery-weight fabric 24˝ × 16˝ for the main part of the bed organizer.

2 Cut 2 pieces of fun coordinating fabric 8½˝ × 12˝ for the pocket.

¡ Let's Make It!

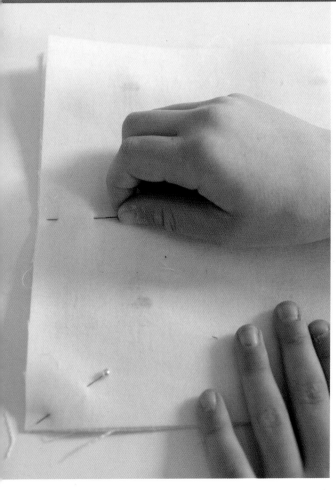

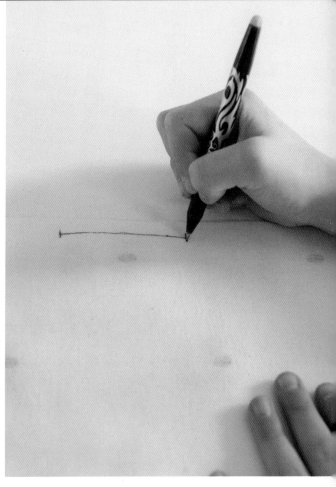

1 Place 2 pocket pieces right sides together, and pin all the way around.

2 Mark a 4˝ no-sew zone with a removable-ink pen along the long edge at the top of the pocket.

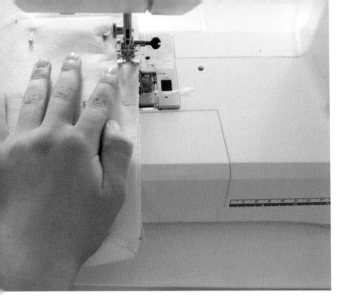

↑ ③ Sew around all 4 sides, with the edge of the foot on the edge of the fabric, but don't forget the no-sew zone!

↑ ④ Pull the pocket right side out through the opening, and iron it nice and flat.

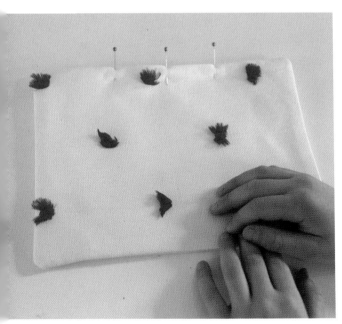

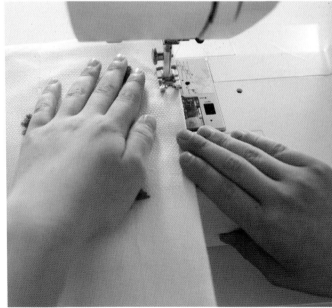

↑ ⑤ Pin the opening closed.

↑ ⑥ Sew the opening closed by sewing nice and close to the edge along the entire length of the long top edge.

↑ **7** Position the pocket on one of the main fabric panels. Center it 3˝ from the short bottom end of the panel, and pin in place. The top of the pocket, with the stitched edge, needs to be facing toward the longer end of the main fabric.

↑ **8** Sew around 3 sides of the pocket. Sew with the edge of the foot on the edge of the fabric, and leave the top of the pocket open.

↑ **9** Put the 2 main fabric panels right sides together, and pin all the way around.

↑ **10** Using the removable-ink pen, mark a 4˝ line on the short side as the no-sew zone.

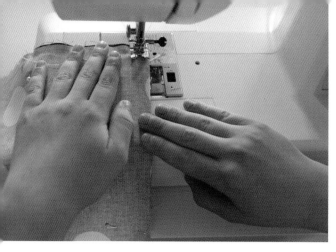

↑ ⑪ Sew around the 4 sides, making sure not to sew in the no-sew zone.

↑ ⑫ Turn right sides out, and push out the corners so they look neat and pointy.

Iron the entire piece so it is lovely and flat.

↑ ⑬ Pin the opening closed.

Think of all the books you can read at once with this nifty organizer!

↑ ⑭ Sew the opening closed by sewing super close to the edge.

⑮ Tuck the long end of the main fabric between your mattress and box spring or under your chair cushion.

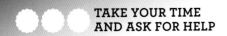
Jewelry Organizer

Finished size: 14¼˝ × 27¾˝

> What Do I Need?

- ½ yard of decorator-weight main fabric
- ½ yard of decorator-weight backing fabric
- 2 sheets of felt, 9˝ × 12˝
- Fun-colored thread
- Removable-ink pen
- Packet of snaps
- 18˝-long dowel
- Piece of ribbon or twine
- Basic supplies (page 12)

> Special Skills

- Refer to The Rules of Sewing (page 9)
- Using an iron (page 21)
- Sewing terms (page 30)

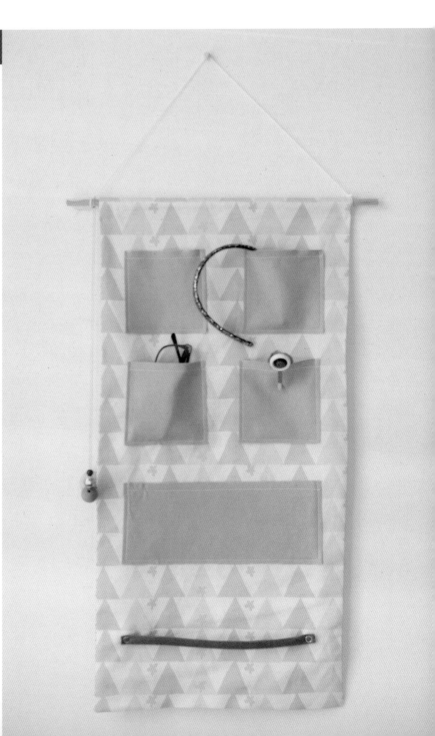

Prepare the Pieces

1 Cut 1 piece of main fabric measuring 15˝ × 30˝.

2 Cut 1 piece of backing fabric measuring 15˝ × 30˝.

3 Cut 4 pockets from felt, each measuring 4½˝ × 4½˝.

4 Cut 1 pocket from felt measuring 4½˝ × 11˝.

5 Cut 1 strip of felt measuring 1½˝ × 11˝.

★ TIP

If you buy 1 yard of decorator fabric, you can use the same fabric on the front and back.

Let's Make It!

1 Thread the machine with a fun-colored thread, and topstitch along the top of all your pocket pieces, with the edge of the presser foot on the edge of the fabric.

2 Take the main fabric panel, and lay it on a nice flat surface. Using the diagram as a reference, lay out all your pocket pieces.

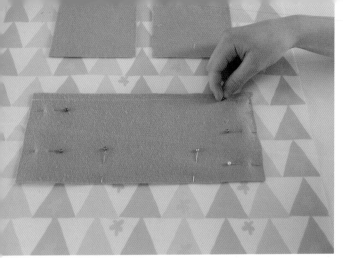

3 Pin all the pockets in place.

4 I use my removable-ink pen to draw a line to follow for a ¼″ seam allowance on the pockets. We want this top stitch to be neat, so drawing it on can sometimes make it a little easier.

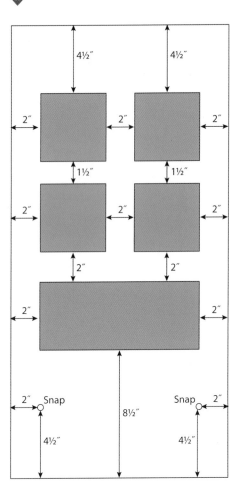

4½″   4½″

2″   2″   2″

1½″   1½″

2″   2″   2″

2″   2″

2″   2″

2″ Snap   Snap 2″

8½″

4½″   4½″

5 Sew around the pockets, following the drawn line and leaving the tops open.

 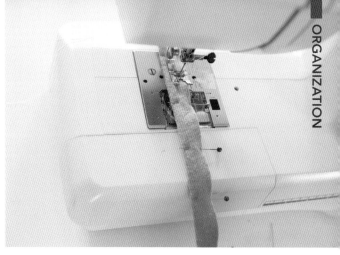

↑ ⑥ Fold the 1½˝-wide strip in half lengthwise, and pin it in place.

↑ ⑦ Sew down the long edge, with the edge of the presser foot on the edge of the fabric.

↑ ⑧ Iron the strip so that the seam is open on the underside.

↑ ⑨ Following the instructions on the snap pack, attach a snap to each end of the ring strip.

↑ ⑩ To determine the location of the other snap halves, lay the ring strip down on the panel, and make little marks on the panel. Check the measurements from the diagram (page 138) as a reference.

↑ ⑪ Attach the other half of the snaps to the panel piece.

↑ ⑫ Take the front and back panels, and pin them right sides together.

↑ ⑬ Use your removable-ink pen to mark a 4˝ line across the top edge to use as the no-sew zone.

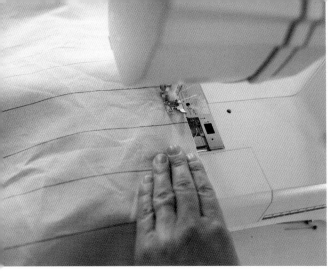

⬆ 14 Sew all 4 sides, with the edge of the presser foot on the edge of the fabric. Don't forget to leave the no-sew zone open!

⬆ 15 Pull the panel right sides out through the opening, and be sure to push out the corners so they look nice and pointy. Give your panel a really good iron.

⬆ 16 Pin the opening closed.

⬆ 17 Sew nice and close to the edge along the opening.

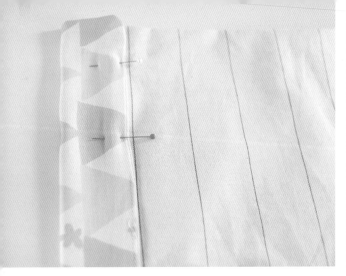

↑ 18 Fold over 1½˝ at the top edge of the fabric panel, and pin in place.

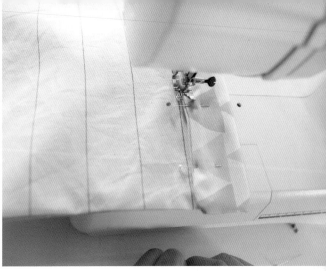

↑ 19 Sew the fold down nice and close to the edge. Remember to backstitch at the beginning and at the end. This creates a casing for your dowel.

↑ 20 Insert the wood dowel into the casing. A little bit should hang out each end. Ask for help to cut it shorter if you need to.

↑ 21 Tie a ribbon or piece of twine to each end of the dowel for hanging, and you are ready to store all your favorite jewelry pieces!

Scrappy Strip Memo Board

Wouldn't you love to have a place to show off all your special things? Sports ribbons, artwork, love letters? This fun and scrappy memo board will be the perfect place to keep all your mementos in one place. Choose a fun color scheme that works well with your room.

Finished size: 23˝ × 17˝

> What Do I Need?

- Strips of fabric in all different widths (Each strip should measure at least 24˝ long.)

- Felt scrap for pocket measuring at least 6˝ × 6˝

- Batting measuring at least 26˝ × 20˝

- Pinking shears

- 1 wood-framed cork memo board measuring 23˝ × 17˝

- Staple gun

- 2 eye screws

- 1 piece of ribbon or twine

- Basic supplies (page 12)

> Special Skills

- Refer to The Rules of Sewing (page 9)

- Using a staple gun (page 24)

- Using an iron (page 21)

- Sewing terms (page 30)

✴ TIP

You can find cork memo boards at most craft and office supply stores. (The sizes may vary a little from what I used.)

Prepare the Pieces

1. Cut a variety of fabric strips in different widths. I cut strips from 1½″ to 4″ wide.

2. Line up your fabric strips in the order that you want to sew them. (It is great to get a visual look at how the fabrics work together before you start sewing.) Cut enough strips to add up to at least 30″ across.

3. Cut a piece of felt 6″ × 6″ for the pocket.

4. Cut a piece of batting 26″ × 20″.

 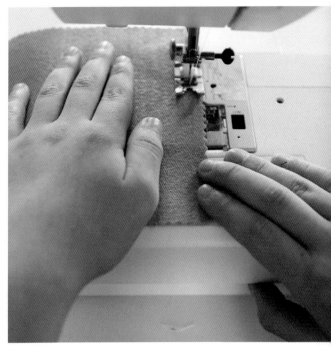

5. Use a pair of pinking shears to give all 4 sides of the pocket a decorative edge.

6. Sew a neat top stitch across the top of the pocket.

¡Let's Make It!

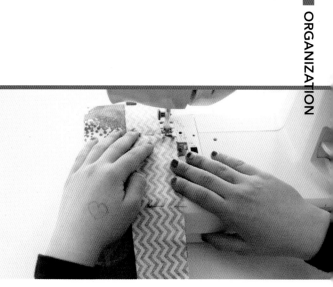

↑ ① Take your first and second strips, and lay them right sides together, matching the long sides. Pin them in place.

↑ ② Sew the pieces together, with the edge of the presser foot on the edge of the fabric.

↑ ③ Iron the strips open.

↑ ④ Attach a third strip in the same way, pin, and sew.

↑ **5** Iron the strips open.

6 Continue sewing the strips until the scrappy strip panel measures at least 28˝ wide. Add more strips if you need to.

↑ **7** Trim the ironed panel down to 28˝ × 22˝.

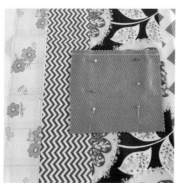

↑ **8** Lay the panel on top of the corkboard to work out the pocket placement.

↑ **9** Position the pocket, and pin it in place.

↑ **10** Sew the pocket in place. Make sure to sew nice and close to the edge, and be sure to leave the top of the pocket open.

¡ Let's Put It All Together!

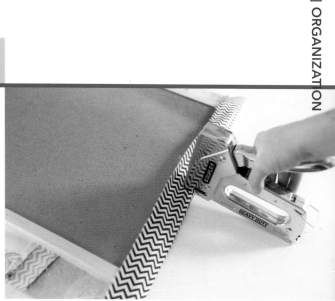

1 Lay the scrappy patch panel right side down on a sturdy flat table.

2 Lay the piece of batting centered on top.

3 Lay the corkboard on the top of the fabric and batting stack. Make sure it is centered.

4 Start by pulling the fabric taut and wrapping it around the edges of the board.

5 Staple in the center of each side edge to hold the fabric in place.

(You may need to ask for help here.)

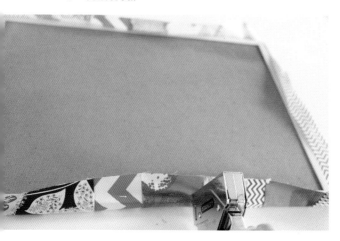

6 Add a couple more staples to both sides of that first staple.

7 Carefully bring the fabric up over the edges of the wooden frame, starting with the corners. Fold in the edges neatly.

8 Staple in place.

9 Continue to staple all the way around, until the board and fabric are super secure!

10 Screw in a pair of eye screws on each side, making sure each screw is the same distance from the top of the frame. String on a piece of ribbon or twine, and you are done!

- ->

Now hang your gorgeous memo board, and admire your handiwork!

Mod Stamped Storage Baskets

From milk crate to awesome storage basket, this project will have you stockpiling forgotten milk crates to create a storage system that even the milkman will be jealous of!

› What Do I Need?

- Canvas fabric measuring 55˝ × 25˝ *
- Fabric square measuring 15˝ × 15˝ *
- Dishwashing sponge
- Scissors
- Large piece of paper or drop cloth
- Fabric paint
- Old towel
- Milk crate (or two!)
- Basic supplies (page 12)

* Size varies depending on the size crate you use. See Prepare the Pieces (page 151).

› Special Skills

- Refer to The Rules of Sewing (page 9)
- Using an iron (page 21)
- Sewing terms (page 30)

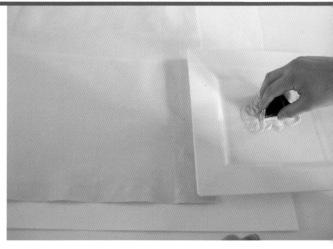

↑ ① Using a sharp pair of scissors, cut the sponge into a fun shape.

↑ ② Lay the canvas fabric on top of a large piece of paper or a drop cloth.

↑ ③ Using the sponge, apply painted shapes all over your piece of canvas.

Wait for the paint to dry for a couple of hours.

④ Lay an old towel over the fabric, and iron the canvas. This will heat set the paint.

Prepare the Pieces

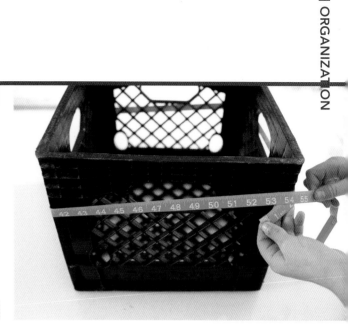

↑ **1** Using a measuring tape, measure from the base of the crate all the way over the top and down to the inside base. Mine measures around 21½˝. Add 1˝ to this, for a total height of 22½˝.

TIP FYI

Milk crates can come in different sizes. I am working with a milk crate that measures 10½˝ tall and 51˝ all around.

↑ **2** Next, take your measuring tape, and measure all the way around the sides. Mine measures 51˝. Add 1½˝ to this, and you'll have a final measurement of 52½˝.

3 Now take a measurement of the inside dimensions of the bottom of the crate. Mine measures 11¾˝ × 11¾˝. Add 1˝ to each measurement and you'll have the final inside measurement; mine is 12¾˝ × 12¾˝.

Let's Sew It!

1 Cut the painted canvas to measure the height and width you calculated. (My measurements are 52½˝ wide × 22½˝ tall.)

2 Cut a square of fabric to measure the inside dimensions you calculated. (My measurements are 12¾˝ × 12¾˝.)

Mod Stamped Storage Baskets **151**

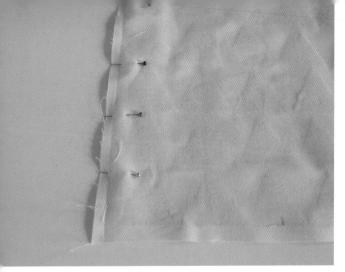 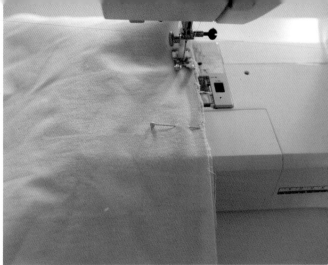

↑ ③ Fold the painted canvas piece in half, and pin the short ends together. Make sure the fabric is folded with right sides together.

↑ ④ Sew with the edge of the fabric along the edge of the presser foot.

 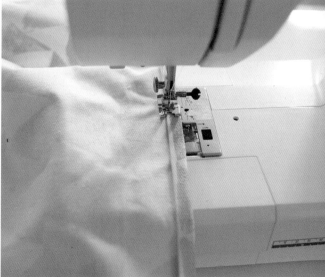

↑ ⑤ On the bottom of the canvas piece, fold up the edge ¼˝ to the wrong side, and iron. Fold it up another ¼˝, iron again, and pin in place.

↑ ⑥ Sew nice and close to the folded edge.

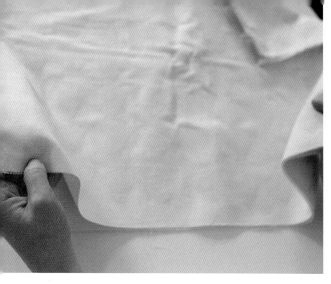

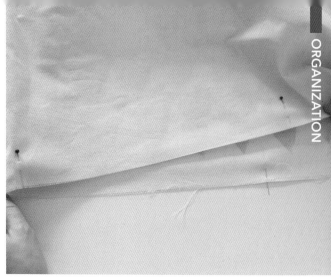

↑ ⑦ Mark the 4 quarter points of the fabric tube. To do this, first fold the tube in half with the seam on one side of the half. Mark the folded edge with a pin. The pin is the halfway point.

↑ ⑧ Now fold the tube in half the other way, matching the seam and pin marks in the center. Mark the folded sides with pins. These are your quarter points.

↑ ⑨ With the right side of the fabric tube and right side of the square together, pin the square corners to the pinned quarter points on the tube.

↑ ⑩ Pin around all the other sides of the square, attaching it to the bottom of the tube.

Mod Stamped Storage Baskets **153**

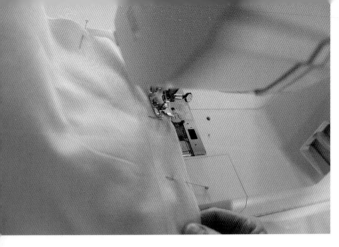

11 Sew carefully around each edge, remembering to move the fabric out of the way when you need to pivot around the corner.

This is quite a tricky thing to do, so take your time and be patient.

12 Turn the tube right side out, and slide the square bottom into the crate. It is going to seem too high for the crate!

13 Now all you need to do is fold the upper part of the tube over the front of the crate.

All done.
Great job!

A TEENY BIT MORE CHALLENGING

Boho Love Lampshade

Imagine how great it will be to have a truly one-of-a-kind lampshade designed by … that's right … you! This easy and fun project will be sure to shine the light on your super craftiness!

> What Do I Need?

- Drum lampshade, any size that will look good with your lamp base

- Large sheet or roll of paper (Kraft paper works well!)

- Pencil

- Fabric scraps

- Hot glue gun

- Trim galore (pompoms, tassels, fringe)

- Basic supplies (page 12)

> Special Skills

- Refer to The Rules of Sewing (page 9)

- Using a hot glue gun (page 23)

- Making and using templates (page 20)

- Using an iron (page 21)

- Sewing terms (page 30)

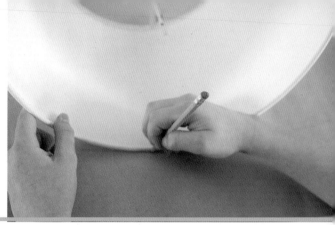

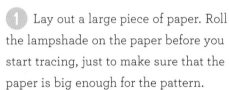
¡ Let's Make the Pattern!

1 Lay out a large piece of paper. Roll the lampshade on the paper before you start tracing, just to make sure that the paper is big enough for the pattern.

2 When you have made sure that the paper is big enough, lay the lampshade on its side on the paper, with the seam touching the paper. Make a mark with your pencil; this will be the starting point.

3 Gently roll the lampshade along the paper, tracing along the bottom edge with your pencil until you get back to the seam.

4 Mark the seam on the paper again. This will be the ending point.

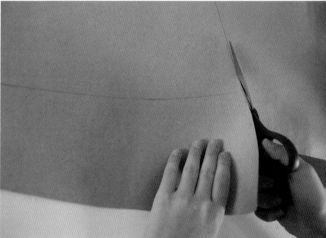

5 Go back to the starting point, and lay the lampshade seam in position. Do the same tracing again, only this time, trace along the top edge of the lampshade.

6 Draw a line on both ends of the pattern, joining the top line to the bottom line.

Yay! You have made the pattern!

7 Cut out the pattern.

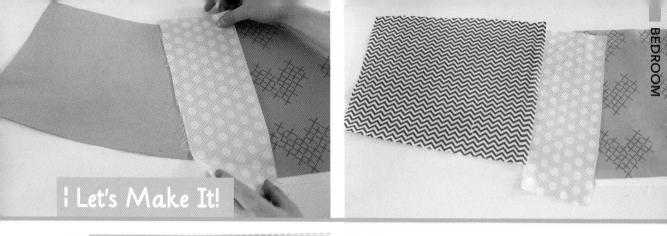

Let's Make It!

Note *There is no exact design for this lampshade. This is a project for you to get creative and design your own work of art.*

1 Choose a few fabric pieces to use to create the design. Lay them out on top of the pattern, and make sure that they are big enough.

It is fun to use thin strips and fat strips of fabric for a fun and unusual look.

2 I like to lay out all the pieces side by side before I start sewing them together.

★ TIP

Always make sure your fabric pieces have nice, straight cut edges before you start sewing them together.

3 Start by laying your first 2 strips right sides together, and pin down the side.

Boho Love Lampshade **157**

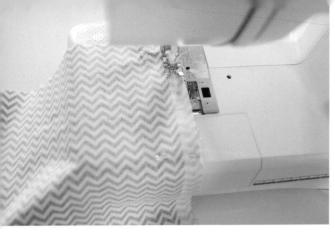

↑ **4** Sew down the side, with the edge of the presser foot on the edge of the fabric.

↑ **5** Iron the strips open.

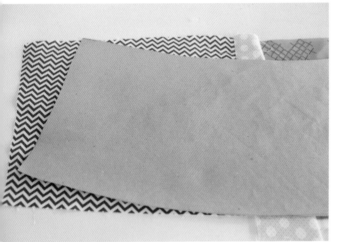

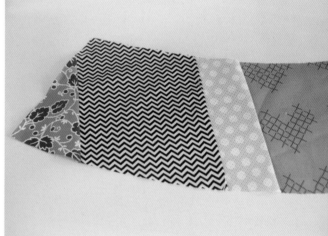

↑ **6** Attach the third piece in the same way.

7 Continue until you have sewn all the pieces together. The piece needs to be bigger than the pattern piece. Add extra strips if you need to.

8 Iron the entire piece.

9 Lay the pattern piece on top of the sewn fabric piece, and pin in place.

↑ **10** Cut out the fabric piece, following the paper pattern and cutting the fabric at least ¼″ longer on one short end.

11 Wrap the fabric piece around the lampshade to check the fit. It's okay if it hangs over the edge a little; we will be able to trim it down later.

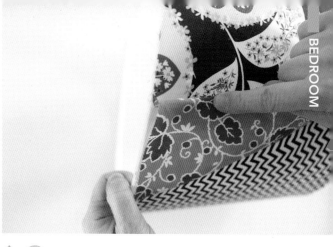

⬆ ⑫ Hot glue one end to the seam of the lampshade. You only need a little bit of glue.

Tightly wrap the fabric around the shade until it meets up and slightly overlaps the start.

⬆ ⑬ Fold over the raw edge a little, and use a few drops of hot glue to hold it in place.

⬆ ⑭ Carefully trim any overhanging fabric from the edges.

✦TIP **Start Adding Trim!**
Here is where you get to be even more crafty and clever. You can choose to add trim to the top, the bottom, or both!

Boho Love Lampshade **159**

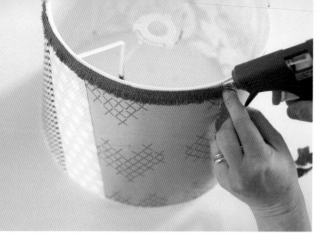

15 Use a little bead of hot glue to attach all the trim. Remember, a little glue goes a long way!

← -

How cool is this lampshade? It will be sure to light up your day (and your room of course!).

Flashy Trash Can

Trash cans should be flashy instead of trashy! Raid your knitting basket for fun yarn to create these one-of-a-kind trash can beauties!

> What Do I Need?

- Hot glue gun
- Variety of yarn
- Small trash can (Mine is 9½˝ tall.)

> Special Skills

- Refer to The Rules of Sewing (page 9)
- Using a hot glue gun (page 23)

¡Let's Make It!

↑ **1** Starting from the bottom of the trash can, apply a line of hot glue all the way around, and wrap your first row of yarn.

↑ **2** Start wrapping tightly around the can. Make sure that the yarn is wrapped really close beside itself rather than on top of itself.

3 Add a few drops of hot glue here and there just to keep things nice and secure.

↑ **4** Work in sections. When you have finished one color, carefully glue the end down before you cut it.

↑ **5** Add the next length of yarn, starting in the same spot where you ended the last yarn, and continue wrapping.

6 When you reach the end, run the hot glue gun all the way around the top of the can to secure your final row.

Try different weights and textures of yarns for a really awesome look!

Isn't your trash can gorgeous?

Simple Window Panel

Don't be daunted by the prospect of sewing drapes. With this easy project, you will be making them for the whole house!

Finished size: 49″ wide × the length you decide on

> What Do I Need?

- 5 squares of quilting fabric measuring 10½″ × 10½″
- Twin-size flat bed sheet
- Basic supplies (page 12)

> Special Skills

- Refer to The Rules of Sewing (page 9)
- Using an iron (page 21)
- Sewing terms (page 30)

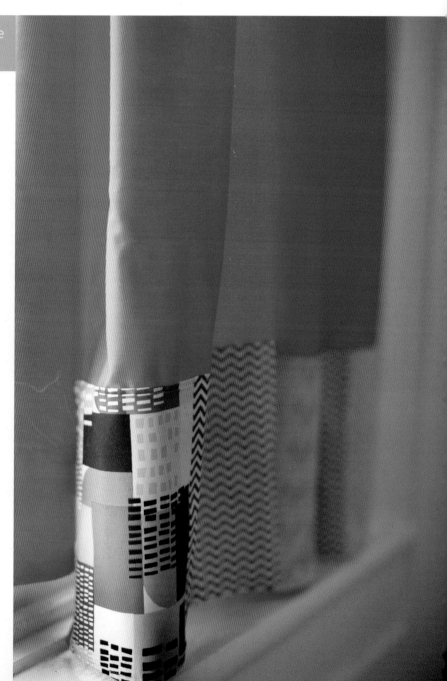

! Prepare the Pieces

1 For each separate curtain panel, you will need a twin flat sheet and 5 squares cut to measure 10½˝ × 10½˝.

2 With an adult's help, measure from your curtain rod to the floor or windowsill.

Add 5½˝ to your measurement. This will be the length you need to cut the sheet.

⁎TIP

Many windows need more than one curtain panel to cover them. Measure the width of your window; if it is more than 36˝ wide, you will need to make 2 curtain panels per window.

3 Cut the sheet so it measures 51˝ wide.

⁎TIP

Remove the hemmed edges when you cut the sheet to size.

! Let's Make It!

THE SHEET

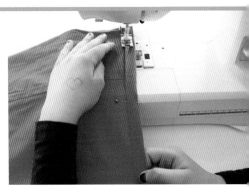

1 Iron the sheet, fold in the long sides of the sheet ½˝ toward the wrong side, fold over again ½˝ toward the wrong side, and iron again.

2 Secure the fold with some pins.

3 Do this with both long sides.

4 Sew nice and close to each folded-in edge.

5 Do the same thing with the bottom of the sheet. You will hem the top edge later.

⁎TIP

Use a thread color to match your fabric color.

THE PATCHWORK

↑ **1** Take 2 of your different fabric squares, and pin them right sides together along one side.

↑ **2** Sew them together, with the edge of the presser foot on the edge of the fabric.

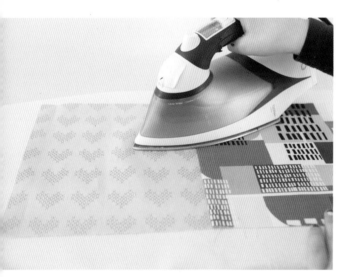

↑ **3** Iron the 2 squares open.

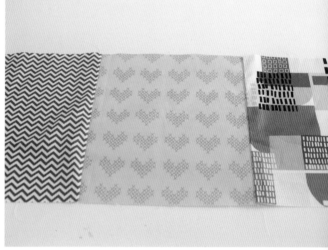

↑ **4** Continue attaching pieces together until you have a row of 5 squares.

5 Fold in the long sides of the patchy strip ¼″, and iron in place. Do this to both long sides.

Fold under the short edges ¼″, and iron in place.

6 You may find that your patchy strip comes out a bit longer than the width of the sheet. Don't worry! Just fold in and iron the short edges to the perfect width!

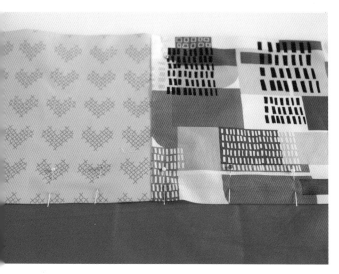

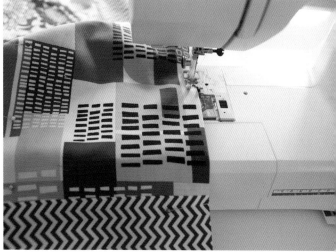

7 Lay the patchy strip along the bottom hemmed edge of the sheet panel, and pin in place, making sure to line the edges up perfectly.

8 Sew the strip in place by stitching close to the edge, down both long sides of the strip.

9 Sew the short ends nice and close to the edge.

Repeat all these steps to create more curtain panels.

Simple Window Panel   **167**

FINISH UP

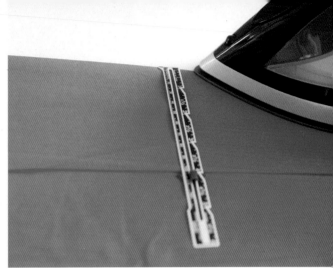

① Fold over the top of the panel ½″, and iron in place.

② Fold over again 4″, and iron.

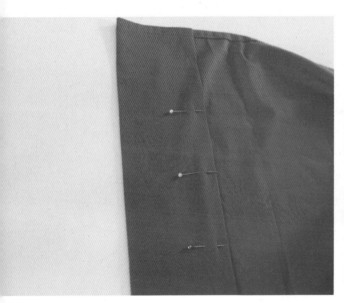

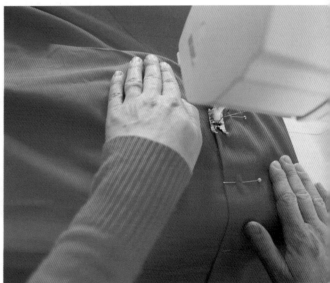

③ Pin in place.

④ Sew nice and close to the folded edge.

⑤ Trim all the loose threads.

With a little help from an adult, slide a curtain rod through the top of your panel, and you're all done! Time to hang your glorious panels. Don't they look fantastic?

Strawberry Patch Bookends

These fun and seriously cute bookends will brighten up even the dreariest bookshelf. Who knew fruit could be so cute?

Finished size: About 9˝ tall

> What Do I Need?

Makes 1 bookend.

- ½ yard of printed quilting cotton
- 10˝ × 10˝ piece of felt for the leaf
- Scrap of felt for the stem
- Embroidery floss to match the felt
- Fiberfill stuffing (Find it at a fabric store.)
- 2 pounds of rice for stuffing
- Sewing machine
- Hot glue gun and glue stick
- Basic supplies (page 12)

> Special Skills

- Refer to The Rules of Sewing (page 9)
- Making and using templates (page 20)
- Sewing a whipstitch (page 28)
- Using a hot glue gun (page 23)

Prepare the Pieces

You'll need the strawberry patterns (pages 236 and 237).

1 Trace both parts of the segment pattern onto parchment paper, and cut it out as one piece. Trace the leaf onto parchment paper.

2 Fold your print fabric in half so the selvage is running down the side. Pin on the strawberry pattern piece. Position it so that it is horizontal across the top of the fabric. Carefully cut it out. Repeat to cut 6 pieces total.

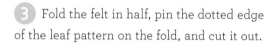

3 Fold the felt in half, pin the dotted edge of the leaf pattern on the fold, and cut it out.

4 Cut a rectangle 1½″ × 4″ of felt for the stem.

Let's Make It!

SEW THE PIECES

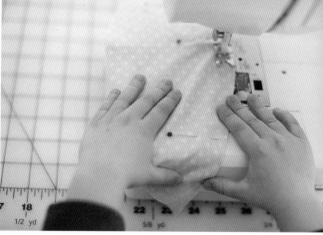

1 Place 2 strawberry pieces right sides together. Pin along one side. The top end of the piece is fatter than the bottom, so make sure the pieces are lined up correctly, with the tops and bottoms matching.

2 With the edge of the presser foot on the edge of the fabric, sew down the length of the strawberry piece. Be careful along the curve. Backstitch at the beginning and again at the end. Repeat Steps 1 and 2 with 2 other pieces.

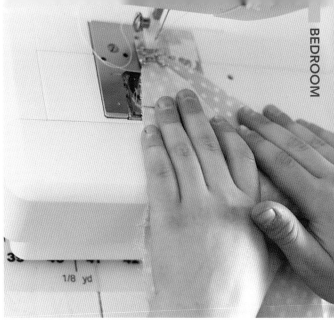

3 Now we're going to attach a third segment to each pair from Step 2. Line up the third segment on one side of one of a pair, making sure the tops are facing in the same direction. Pin carefully, and sew. Again, repeat this with the other pair. This is a little tricky, so sew like a snail! You now have 2 half-strawberries.

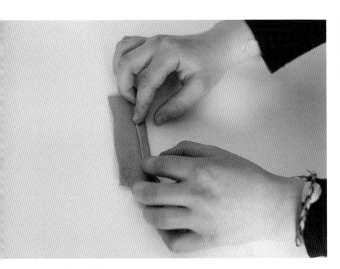
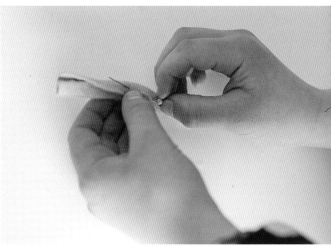

4 To sew the stem, carefully roll up the piece of felt. Secure it with a pin so it stays tight.

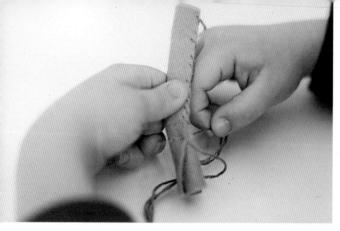

↑ **5** Thread an embroidery needle with matching embroidery thread. Sew a whip-stitch to secure the stem. Remember to start with a knot.

↑ **6** Center the stem at the top of a half-strawberry. Remember, the top is the fatter end. Pin the stem to the right (patterned) side of the fabric. Make sure it is pointing down. If you get stuck, look at the photo as a guide. Secure the stem with a pin.

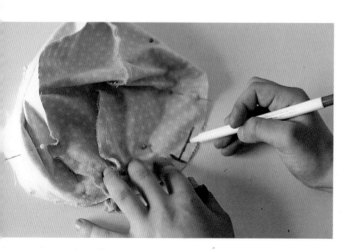

↑ **7** Place the strawberry halves right sides together, and carefully pin the edges around the whole strawberry. Mark a 2″ gap for stuffing close to the top with your disappearing-ink marker.

↑ **8** Sew around the strawberry.

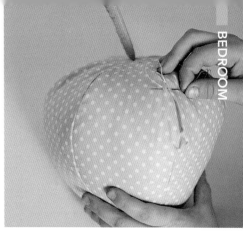

PUT IT TOGETHER

① Very carefully turn the strawberry right side out. Time to raid the pantry! Ask an adult to help you hold the hole open, and fill the strawberry one-third to one-half full with rice. Use a rolled-up piece of paper or a funnel for this part.

② Using small tufts of fiberfill, start stuffing the rest of the strawberry. Make sure to fill every little nook and cranny.

③ Thread a sewing needle with button thread. Sew up the hole using a whipstitch.

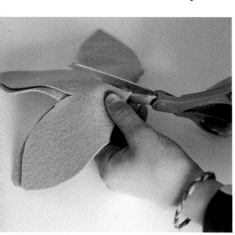

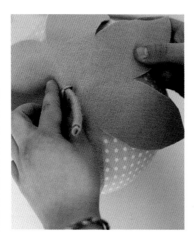

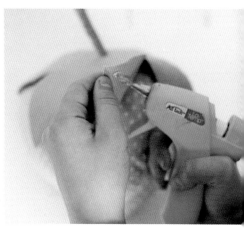

④ Fold the leaf piece in half, and carefully snip a tiny hole right in the center.

⑤ Place the leaf on top of the strawberry, and pull the stem through the hole.

Put a dab of hot glue on the tips of the strawberry leaves. Press them in place until the glue is dry.

Ta-da! Take a break. When you are ready, come back and make number 2 of our bookend pair.

Pillows: Three Ways

For this project, we will be using one simple pillow pattern and working on three different decorative techniques to create our own fabric! The great thing about it—they all look fab piled high on your bed!

Finished size: 19¼˝ × 19¼˝

Paint Splatter Pillow

Who said that splattered paint = mess? These splattered pillows are the perfect artwork for your room.

❯ What Do I Need?

- ¾ yard of natural canvas fabric, at least 54˝ wide

- Drop cloth

- 1 small bottle of fabric paint

- Plastic disposable bowl

- Spoon

- Iron

- Old towel

- Clothes you can get messy

❯ Special Skills

- Refer to The Rules of Sewing (page 9)

- Using an iron (page 21)

Let's Make It!

We need to start by cutting our front pillow panel.

1 Cut a 20″ × 20″ square of canvas fabric.

2 Lay your drop cloth down somewhere outside.

3 Lay the canvas fabric on top of the drop cloth.

4 Pour paint into a little bowl.

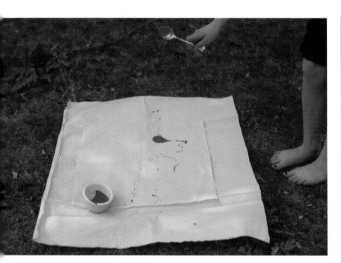

5 Splatter paint onto the canvas fabric using the spoon to flick the paint. Be sure you're wearing clothes that can get messy.

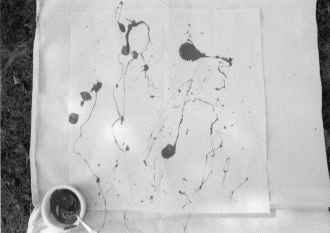

6 When you are happy with your work, leave the canvas to dry overnight.

7 When the canvas is totally dry, you can lay an old towel over the painted area, and run an iron over it. This will set the paint.

8 Skip to Time to Make the Pillows! (page 183) to finish your pillow.

Bleached-Out Heart Pillow

So bleach conjures up images of scrubbing the floor? Let's look at its powers in another way by creating an awesome bleached heart effect on denim.

> What Do I Need?

- ¾ yard of dark denim fabric, at least 54″ wide
- Drop cloth
- Removable-ink pen
- Plastic disposable bowl
- Small cup of bleach
- Old paintbrush
- Washing machine
- Apron or old clothes
- Iron

> Special Skills

- Refer to The Rules of Sewing (page 9)
- Using an iron (page 21)

¡ Let's Make It!

We need to start by cutting our front pillow panel.

1 Cut a 20˝ × 20˝ square of denim fabric.

2 In an open, well-ventilated area, lay down a drop cloth to protect your work area.

3 Place your denim fabric with the right side facing up.

4 Draw a heart shape using your removable-ink pen. (It looks best if it is centered on the square.)

*TIP

You can use the heart-shape pattern (page 232) to create a parchment paper pattern (see Making and Using Templates, page 20) or draw the heart freehand.

5 Pour bleach into the plastic bowl. Make sure you are wearing an apron and working in a well-ventilated area because bleach has harmful fumes.

*TIP Caution!

Bleach is a dangerous chemical, so you should use caution and ask for help when using it. Always make sure you use bleach outside or in a well-ventilated room. Also, make sure you wear an apron or some old clothes when you are using bleach; it can really damage your clothes if it splashes on them. If you happen to get bleach on your hands, be sure to wash them well right away. It's always a good idea to read the caution note on the bleach bottle.

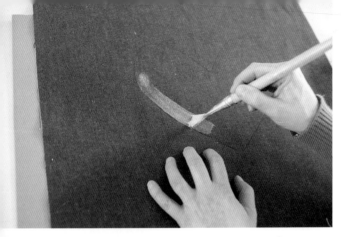

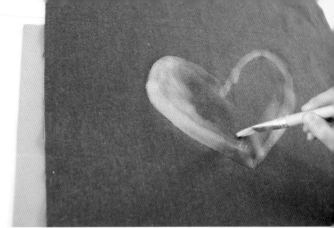

↑ ⑥ Dip your paintbrush into the bleach, and starting at the outside edge, evenly paint your heart with the bleach.

↑ You should paint over the area a couple of times.

∴★TIP

Don't leave bleach on the denim for more than 30 minutes. The bleach can eat through the fabric, and instead of a heart, you will find a hole!

↑ ⑦ Leave the fabric for 30 minutes; the heart should have become very pale and bleached out.

⑧ Throw your piece of fabric in the washing machine and ask an adult to turn on the cold cycle. After the wash, throw it in the dryer.

⑨ Give it a good iron.

Skip to Time to Make the Pillows! (page 183); now you're ready to finish the pillow!

Painted Chevron Pillow

Masking tape isn't only for painting your room! You can also use it to paint a fun, mod pillow. Yay for masking tape!

> What Do I Need?

- ¾ yard of patterned fabric, at least 54″ wide (I like gingham for this project.)

- Removable-ink pen

- Ruler

- 1″-wide masking tape

- Drop cloth or paper to cover surface

- Fabric paint

- Sponge brush for stenciling

- Old towel or pressing cloth

- Iron

> Special Skills

- Refer to The Rules of Sewing (page 9)

- Using an iron (page 21)

Let's Make It!

We need to start by cutting our front pillow panel.

1 Cut a 20˝ × 20˝ square of patterned fabric.

2 Using the ruler and removable-ink pen, mark 4 columns, each measuring 5˝ wide.

3 Do the same thing but across the fabric in 4 rows, 5˝ wide. Let's call each of these sections blocks.

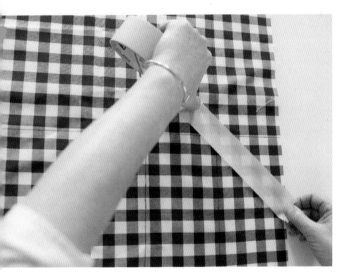

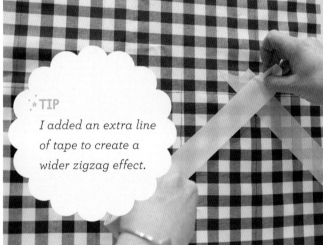

TIP

I added an extra line of tape to create a wider zigzag effect.

4 Using the block corners as your guide, apply the center of the masking tape to the center of the lower right corner, and run it to the top center of the first block.

5 Do the opposite with the next piece of tape to create a zigzag effect.

6 Continue until you have made 4 lines of taped zigzags across the fabric square.

↑ ⑦ Iron the panel to remove any ink.

↑ ⑧ Trim off any overhanging masking tape to make sharp lines.

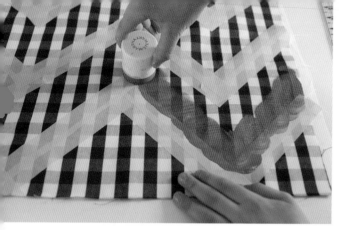
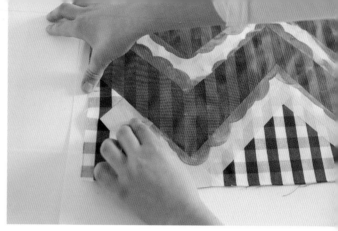

↑ ⑨ Lay the pillow front on a flat surface on top of a drop cloth or paper.

⑩ Using the sponge stenciling brush, apply the paint, making sure to use a tapping up-and-down motion around the masking tape area.

↑ ⑪ Leave the pillow front to dry for about an hour before removing the tape.

⑫ Wait another hour; then cover the painted area with an old towel or pressing cloth, and iron the design. ↓

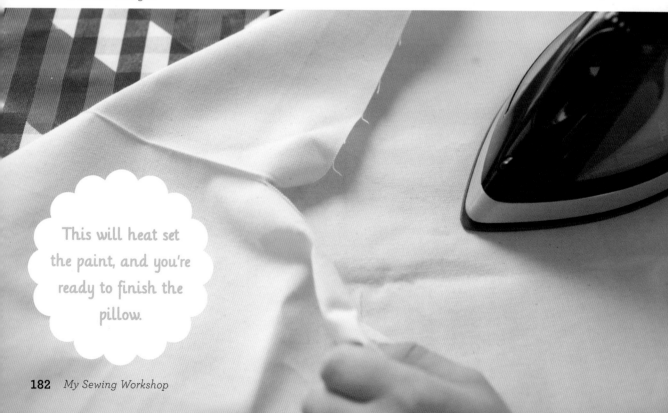

This will heat set the paint, and you're ready to finish the pillow.

Time to Make the Pillows!

Now that you have created the pillow fronts, it's time to make the pillows!

> What Do I Need?

- The remaining piece of fabric
- Pinking shears
- 20″ pillow form, 1 for each pillow
- Basic supplies (page 12)

> Special Skills

- Refer to The Rules of Sewing (page 9)
- Sewing terms (page 30)

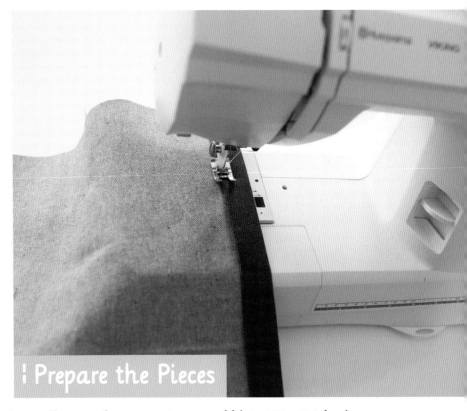

¦ Prepare the Pieces

You have already cut your front pillow panel. Now cut 2 pieces of fabric 15″ × 20″ for the pillow back.

¦ Let's Make It!

1 On a pillow back piece, fold over the edge of a long side about ½″. Iron along this fold.

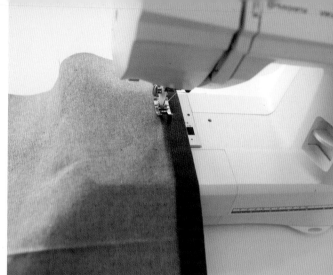

↑ **②** Fold it over again, iron the fold, and pin it in place.

Repeat this with the second back piece.

↑ **③** Sew down the fold on both pieces. Try to sew close to the edge of the first fold.

④ Lay the pillow front faceup, and lay a back piece facedown on top of the front piece. Be sure to line up the raw edges along the top, bottom, and one side.

⑤ Now lay the second back piece facedown on the stack. This time, make sure that the piece is lined up with the other side of the pillow front. The 2 back pieces will overlap with the hemmed edges toward the center.

------------------------------------>

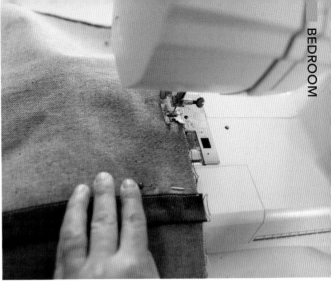

↑ ⑥ Pin everything in place.

↑ ⑦ Sew around all 4 sides, with the edge of the presser foot on the edge of the fabric.

⑧ Trim the corners and trim around the edges with pinking shears to prevent fraying. Turn the pillow right side out.

⑨ Iron the pillow cover.

⑩ Insert the pillow form.

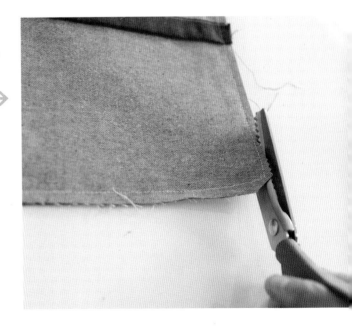

Voila! How easy was that?
Time to make a whole stack of pillows for your space!

Olive Owl

There's nothing like a cute owl stuffie to make your day a little brighter. Olive will be perfectly happy perched on your bed or on a cozy shelf. Hoot! Hoot!

Finished size: 11″ × 13″

> What Do I Need?

- ½ yard of bright printed quilting cotton or lightweight decorator fabric for the body

- Scrap of quilting cotton measuring at least 7″ × 7″ for the wings

- Felt scraps in different colors for the inner eyes, outer eyes, beak, feet, feathers, and wings

- 2 large buttons for the eyes

- Fiberfill stuffing (Find it at a fabric store.)

- Sewing machine

- Basic supplies (page 12)

> Special Skills

- Refer to The Rules of Sewing (page 9)

- Making and using templates (page 20)

- Sewing a whipstitch (page 28)

- Sewing on a button (page 25)

- Using an iron (page 21)

¡ Prepare the Pieces

You'll need the owl patterns (pages 232–235).

1 Enlarge the body patterns, and then trace the enlargements onto parchment paper and cut them out. Tape the enlarged body bottom pattern to the enlarged body top pattern along the straight edge to make a whole body pattern.

2 Fold your piece of cotton fabric so that the right sides are together.

3 Pin the body pattern on the fabric, and then cut out the pattern pieces. You will have the front and back of the owl.

4 Cut 2 large circles of felt for Olive's outer eyes.

5 Cut 2 smaller circles of felt for Olive's inner eyes.

6 Cut 1 beak from felt.

7 Cut 2 feet pieces from felt.

8 Cut 1 of each feather piece from felt.

9 Cut 2 wing pieces from felt and 2 wing pieces from cotton fabric.

¡ Let's Make It!

BODY

1 Place the beak on the owl's front body. (Look at the pattern or the project photo to see where it goes.) Pin the beak in place, and sew it on, stitching close to the edge.

> **TIP Extra Help**
> *You may want to use fusible web to hold the beak in place before you sew. If you do, see Using Paper-Backed Fusible Web (page 22).*

↑ ② Place the row of 3-pointed feathers on Olive's front body. Pin it in place.

↑ ③ Sew across the top of the feathers. Sew nice and close to the edge. Repeat to sew the smaller row of feathers overlapping the first row.

↑ ④ Put Olive's front and back body pieces right sides together. Pin them all the way around. Mark a 3˝ line with your disappearing-ink marker at the bottom of Olive. This will be the hole you use to stuff her.

↑ ⑤ With the edge of the presser foot on the edge of the fabric, sew all the way around. Stop at the beginning of the 3˝ line. Start again at the other end. Be sure to backstitch at each start and stop. Sew carefully on the tight curves of Olive's ears. You want them to be pointy.

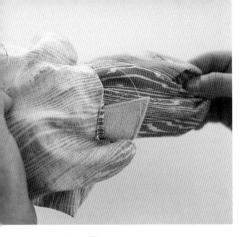

↑ 6 Turn her right side out.

↑ 7 Using small tufts of fiberfill, start stuffing Olive. Make sure you get enough stuffing in her ears!

↑ 8 Using your best whipstitch, hand stitch the hole closed.

↑ 9 Time to add the eyes. I like to cut slits around the outside of both the outer and the inner eye. But you can leave them plain if you like.

↑ 10 Sew on a button for each eye, with the felt eye pieces stacked underneath. Look at the pattern for placement.

WINGS AND FEET

↑ ① Let's tackle the wings! With 1 piece of felt and 1 piece of fabric right sides together, pin all the way around each wing.

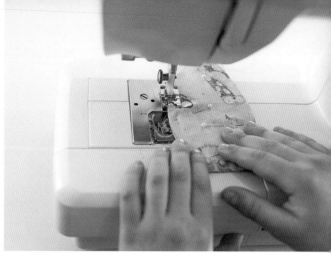

↑ ② Sew around each wing piece, but leave the straight edge open. Sew with the edge of the presser foot on the edge of the fabric.

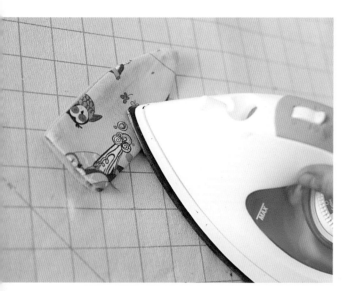

↑ ③ Turn both wings right side out, and iron them. Fold in the open edges about ¼″, and iron them nice and flat.

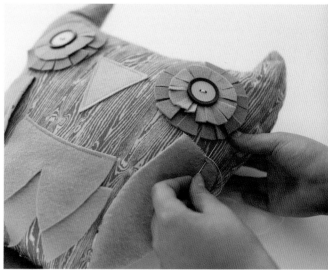

↑ ④ Position the wings on the sides of Olive's body, and carefully hand stitch them on. Don't forget to tie a knot at the beginning and at the end!

She is really starting to look like an owl, don't you think?

5 Now let's sew on those cute little feet! Position them on the underside of Olive's body. Pin them in place. Using button thread, carefully sew them on. Sew along the straight edge of the feet only.

← – – – – – – – – – – – – – – – – – –

All done. I think she needs a friend, don't you? This is a great project to experiment with different fabrics and colors. Make it yours!

Olive Owl **191**

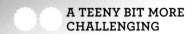
Simple Patch Throw

*There is nothing better on a chilly night than to snuggle up in a cozy quilt.
This quilt will not only be cozy but also be made by you! How cool is that?*

Finished size: 43¾˝ × 52½˝

> What Do I Need?

- 30 fabric squares measuring
  9½˝ × 9½˝

- Cotton quilt batting
  measuring at least 45˝ × 54˝

- 1½-yard piece of fabric for
  the backing

- Removable-ink pen

- Yarn

- Embroidery needle

- Basic supplies (page 12)

> Special Skills

- Refer to The Rules of Sewing
  (page 9)

- Using an iron (page 21)

- Sewing terms (page 30)

Prepare the Pieces

1 Cut 30 fabric squares, from all different fabrics, each measuring 9½˝ × 9½˝.

2 Cut the batting to measure 45˝ × 54˝.

3 Cut the backing fabric to measure 45˝ × 54˝.

⋆TIP

I usually like to cut my squares from a variety of print fabrics, approximately 5 squares from each print.

Let's Make It!

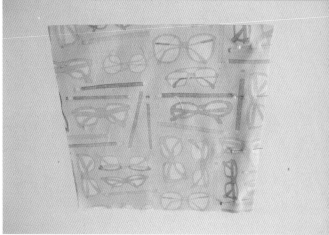

1 Lay out your 9½˝ fabric squares so that the design is positioned the way you want it, with 5 squares across and 6 squares down.

2 Working in rows, take your first 2 squares, lay them right sides together, and pin one side.

3 Sew with the edge of the presser foot on the edge of the fabric.

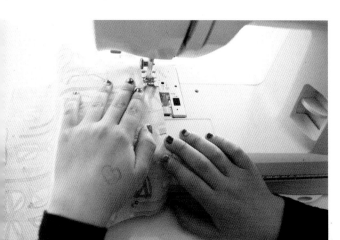

▲ ④ Iron the squares open.

⑤ Repeat Steps 2–4 (page 193 and above) until an entire row of 5 squares is sewn together and ironed.

▲ ⑥ Do the same thing with all your squares so that you end up with a total of 6 patch rows.

⋆TIP

I like to pin a little piece of paper to the first square of each row. I number each piece of paper so that I don't forget which row goes where.

▲ ⑦ Take your first and second rows, and lay them right sides together, being sure to match the seams. Pin in place.

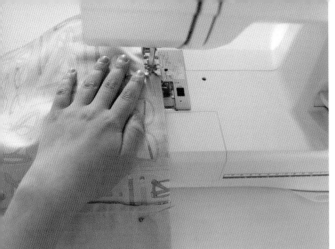

⑧ Sew the long edge of the 2 rows together, with the edge of the presser foot on the edge of the fabric.

⑨ Iron the rows open.

⑩ Continue doing this until all the rows are sewn together.

⑪ Give it one final iron, and you are done with this part!

Let's Put It All Together!

① Lay the batting on a large flat surface.

② Lay the patchwork top right side up on top of the batting. Using the patchwork top as the guide, cut around the batting to make it the same size. Set the batting aside.

③ Lay the backing right side up and lay the patchwork top right side down on the backing. Using the top as a guide, cut the backing to the correct size.

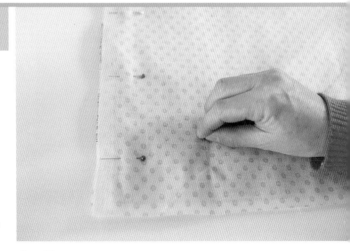

④ Now lay the batting on top of the layered backing and patchwork top from Step 3. Make sure the edges are even, and pin all the way around.

Simple Patch Throw **195**

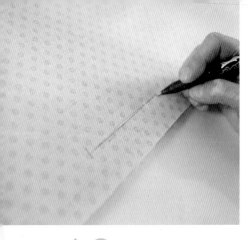
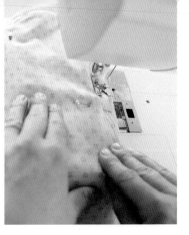

⬆ **5** Mark a 4″ line on one side of the throw. This will be our no-sew zone. We will need this hole to turn the throw right side out!

⬆ **6** With the edge of the presser foot on the edge of the fabric, sew all the way around the 4 sides of the throw. *Remember:* Don't sew in the no-sew zone!

⬆ **7** Reach between the 2 layers of fabric, and pull the throw right side out through the hole. Make sure the batting remains in the center.

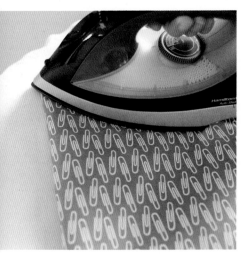
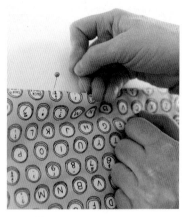
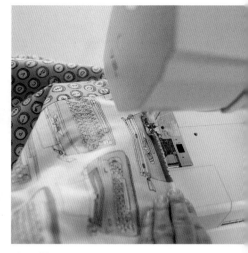

⬆ **8** Push out all the corners, and give it a really good iron.

⬆ **9** Turn the raw edges of the hole to the inside. Pin the hole closed.

⬆ **10** Sew up the hole with the sewing machine. Sew nice and close to the edge.

11 Use the iron to remove the ink.

¡ Let's Tie It!

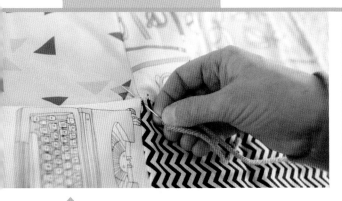

Tying a throw is a great way to hold all the layers together, and it also looks super cute!

1 Cut an arm's length of fun yarn and thread it onto a sharp embroidery needle.

2 At a patchwork square corner, bring the needle down through all the layers and then up again right beside where you started.

3 Tie a double knot in your yarn.

4 Cut off the yarn ends to approximately ½˝–1˝.

5 Tie a knot in the corner of each of the patchwork squares. Keep going until you are done.

Hooray! Doesn't your throw look amazing?

Hippy Dippy Bed Canopy

Turn your bedroom into a dreamy hideaway with this easy-peasy bed canopy. I feel relaxed just thinking about it!

> What Do I Need?

- 5½ yards of a thin 60˝-wide cotton fabric

- Wood embroidery hoop measuring 23˝ across

- Pencil

- Sashing cord or clothesline

- Basic supplies (page 12)

> Special Skills

- Refer to The Rules of Sewing (page 9)

- Using an iron (page 21)

- Sewing terms (page 30)

¦ Prepare the Pieces

1 Cut 2 fabric panels, each measuring 55˝ × 84˝.

2 Cut 10 fabric strips measuring 4½˝ × 27˝.

¦ Let's Make It!

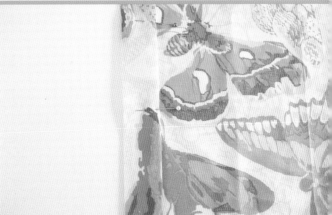

1 For each of the fabric panels, fold in a long edge of the fabric 1˝ to the wrong side, and iron. Fold in another 1˝, and iron again.

2 Pin in place.

3 Do the same with the other long side.

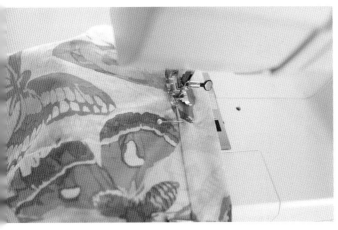

4 Sew nice and close to the first folded edge down each long side of the panels.

5 Fold in the top and bottom edges of the fabric 1˝ to the wrong side, and iron. Fold in another 1˝, iron again, and pin in place.

Hippy Dippy Bed Canopy **199**

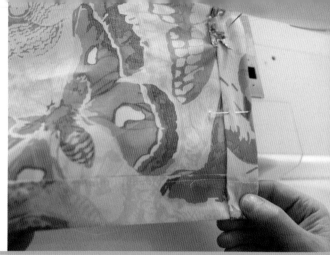

6 Once again, you will be sewing nice and close to the first folded edge down each top and bottom edge of the panels.

Your panels should measure approximately 51˝ × 80˝.

-->

NOW FOR THE TIES

1 Take one of the strips, and fold it in half lengthwise, wrong sides together. Iron it nice and flat.

2 Open the strip, fold each of the short ends in about ¼˝ to the wrong side, and iron.

3 Fold each of the long ends in about ¼˝ to the wrong side, and iron.

4 Refold the entire strip in half again, and iron.

5 You may want to pin down the open edges, especially if you are using a thin fabric.

-->

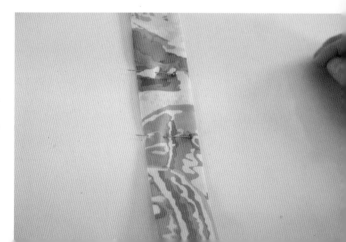

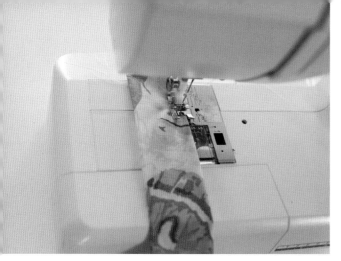

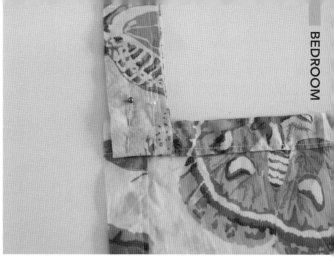

(6) Sew nice and close to the folded edge down both the short ends and the long side.

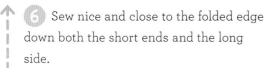

(7) Repeat Steps 1–6 (previous page and above) to make 10 ties.

(8) Fold a tie in half, and pin the folded end onto one top corner of a panel. Repeat to pin a folded tie to both corners of the panel.

(9) Now measure with your ruler to find the halfway point of the top of the panel, and pin another tie.

(10) Next, find the halfway point between the end and middle ties, and pin your fourth tie.

Do the same on the other side with the final tie.

(11) Sew along the folded edge of each tie. Make sure to backstitch at the beginning and end.

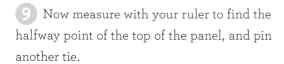

(12) Repeat Steps 8–11 (above) with the other panel.

★ TIP

Backstitching is crucial to keep your stitching nice and tight!

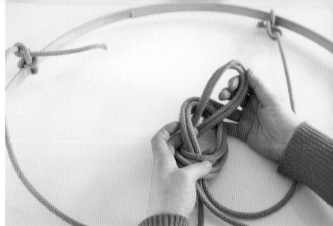

FINISH UP

1 Mark the quarter points of the hoop with a pencil. This is where we will be tying the cord to hang the canopy. The cord needs to be perfectly positioned so the canopy does not tilt unevenly.

2 Tie a long length of sashing cord or clothesline with a triple knot at each of the pencil points.

3 Hold the canopy up from the cord, and adjust the cord lengths until the hoop is hanging perfectly level.

4 Tie a knot in the top.

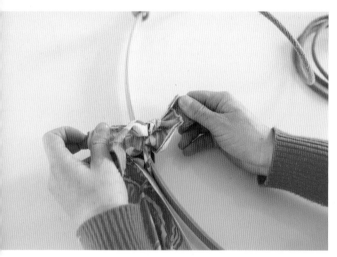

5 Tie the panels to the embroidery hoop. Make the knots loose enough to be able to slide them on the hoop so you can adjust the panels later.

Ready to hang!

★TIP
The length of the cord will depend on how high your ceiling is. This is a good time to ask for help from an adult.

Large Patch Headboard

What better place to lay your head than against your very own, super custom patch headboard! Your friends will be asking where on earth you got it, and you can proudly tell them, "I made it!"

Finished size: 30˝ × 40˝

> What Do I Need?

- 20 fabric squares measuring 10½˝ × 10½˝

- 12 self-covering buttons, size 2˝

- Small scraps of fabric for the self-covering buttons

- 2 pieces of low-loft batting measuring 32˝ × 42˝

- Stretched artist canvas measuring 30˝ × 40˝

- Staple gun

- Button thread

- Basic supplies (page 12)

> Special Skills

- Refer to The Rules of Sewing (page 9)

- Sewing on a button (page 25)

- Using a staple gun (page 24)

- Using an iron (page 21)

- Sewing terms (page 30)

Large Patch Headboard **203**

Prepare the Pieces

1. Cut 20 squares from different fabrics, each measuring 10½″ × 10½″.

(For this project, I like using at least 2 of each print.)

2. Following the instructions on the packet, make 12 size 2″ covered buttons.

Let's Make It!

THE PATCHWORK

1. Lay out your fabric squares with 5 squares across and 4 squares down.

2. Working in rows, take your first 2 squares, lay them right sides together, and pin.

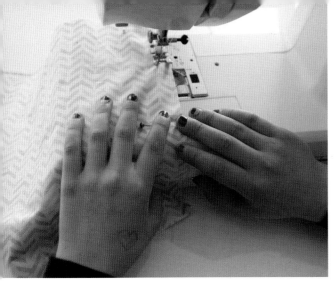

↑ ③ Sew the 2 squares together, with the edge of the presser foot on the edge of the fabric.

↑ ④ Iron the squares open.

↑ ⑤ Repeat these steps until the entire row of 5 squares is sewn together and ironed.

↑ ⑥ Do this with all your rows so that you end up with 4 patch rows.

7 Take your first and second rows, and lay them right sides together, being sure to match the seams. Pin in place.

8 Sew the long edge of the 2 rows together, with the edge of the foot on the edge of the fabric.

9 Iron the rows open.

10 Continue doing this until all the rows are sewn together.

11 Give it one final iron, and you are done with the patchwork panel!

Let's Put It All Together!

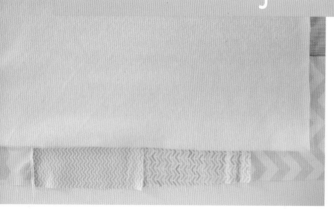

1 Lay your patchwork panel right side down on a large flat surface.

2 Center the 2 pieces of batting on top of the patchwork panel.

3 Lay the stretched artist canvas right side down in the center of the patchwork and batting stack.

★TIP

You may want to use a ruler to measure around the fabric edges. Make sure that the canvas is perfectly centered on the patchy panel.

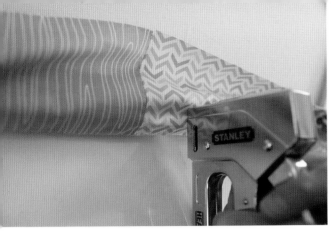

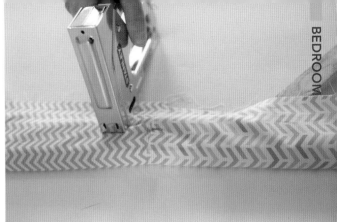

4 Start by wrapping the fabric and batting tightly around the edges of the canvas.

5 With help from a parent or grown-up, use the staple gun to put an anchoring staple in the center of each side edge of the frame. Staple through the fabric, batting, and frame to hold the layers in place.

6 Staple on each side of those initial anchoring staples.

Time to tackle the corners.

7 First, pull the fabric over the corner, and anchor it with a staple.

Then, gently fold the fabric in on either side of that point, and staple into place.

8 Continue stapling around the rest of the canvas until everything is nice and secure.

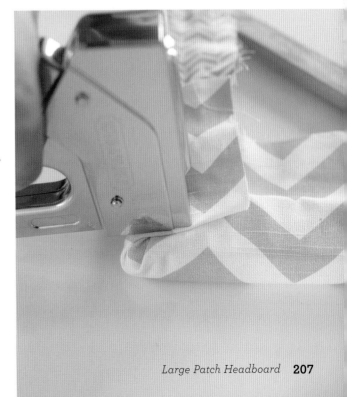

THE TUFTING

↑ **1** Using a sharp needle threaded with button thread, push the needle from behind through the canvas at the point where the patch squares intersect.

↑ **2** Push the needle through the loop underneath the covered button.

↑ **3** Push the needle back down through to the back of the canvas.

↑ **4** Tie a tight triple knot, and trim the threads.

↑ **5** Continue to do this, sewing all your buttons to the headboard.

All done! You can easily hang this lightweight headboard on a couple of nails in the wall!

How awesome and professional does your headboard look?

EASY PEASY

Squeaky Dog Bone

I'm sure your pup loves to play and chew his toys all day long. Think how much she will love to chew on a toy made by you!

This is a great project to make for your four-legged friend, or you could even grab a group of friends and make a stack for your local SPCA or animal shelter!

> What Do I Need?

- ¼ yard of canvas-type fabric
- Dog toy squeaker (available at pet stores and online)
- Polyester stuffing
- Basic supplies (page 12)

> Special Skills

- Refer to The Rules of Sewing (page 9)
- Using an iron (page 21)
- Making and using templates (page 20)
- Sewing a whipstitch (page 28)
- Sewing around a corner (page 19)

Prepare the Pieces

You'll need the dog bone pattern (page 238).

1 Use the dog bone pattern to cut 1 complete bone piece from the canvas fabric. The pattern shows only half a bone. To make a full bone template, fold a large piece of paper in half, place the fold on the dotted center line of the pattern, and trace. Cut out the template and open it up.

2 Cut another piece of canvas to measure 8″ × 15″ for the backing.

Let's Make It!

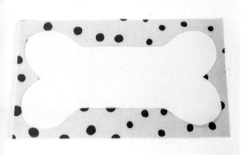 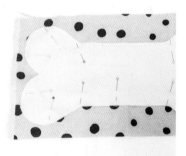 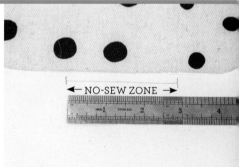

NO-SEW ZONE

1 Lay the fabric bone on top of the backing fabric with right sides together and pin in place.

2 Mark a 3″ no-sew zone along a straight edge of the bone (refer to the pattern piece for the markings).

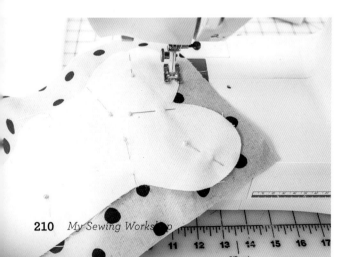

3 Sew all the way around with the edge of the presser foot on the edge of the fabric. Make sure not to sew in the no-sew zone! There are lots of curves here, so be sure to sew slowly and pivot carefully when you are sewing around the sharp corners in both ends.

↑ ④ Carefully cut around the bone to remove the excess backing fabric.

↑ ⑤ Use the tips of the scissors to snip every 1˝ around the curved section of the bone. This will help the bone keep its curved shape when you pull it right side out. Be very careful not to clip into the stitching!

↑ ⑥ Pull the bone right side out, making sure to push out all the little nooks and crannies.

↑ ⑦ Tightly stuff each end of the bone with stuffing.

↑ ⑧ When you have added ¾ of the stuffing, stop and pop the squeaker through the hole. Continue stuffing, making sure there is stuffing all around the squeaker.

↑ ⑨ Pin the opening closed.

⑩ Carefully whip-stitch the opening closed with button thread and securely knot the thread at the end.

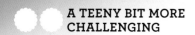
Kitty Catnip Toy

You cannot go wrong with this fishy-shaped kitty toy! Add some catnip and it will be your kitty's favorite plaything!

> What Do I Need?

- 6˝ × 8˝ piece of felt for each fish body
- 5˝ × 5˝ piece of felt for the scales of 1 fish
- Colored embroidery floss for the eyes
- ¼˝ or ½˝ dowel (can be purchased at a craft or hardware store)
- Dried catnip (can be purchased at a pet supply store)
- Polyester stuffing
- Approximately 24˝ of twine
- Fun-colored sewing machine thread
- Basic supplies (page 12)

> Special Skills

- Refer to The Rules of Sewing (page 9)
- Using an iron (page 21)
- Making and using templates (page 20)
- Sewing a Vicki knot (page 29)

Prepare the Pieces

You'll need the kitty toy patterns (page 239).

1 Use the patterns to make templates.

2 Cut 2 fish bodies for each fish.

3 Cut 8 sets of scales for each fish.

Let's Make It!

1 Measure 2″ from the top point of the fish body and draw a line.

2 Draw 3 more lines, each ½″ under the previous line. You should now have 4 lines. These are the fish-scale placement lines.

3 Place a row of fish scales under the bottom line and stitch in place across the top of the scales.

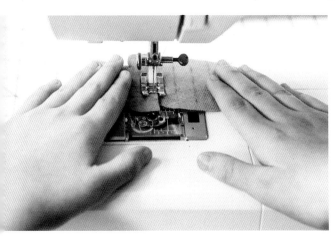 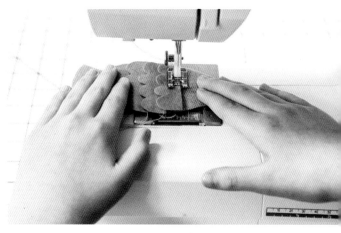

4 Attach another row of scales under the next line.

5 Continue until you have 4 rows of scales sewn onto the fish body. I used a fun zigzag stitch for the top set of scales.

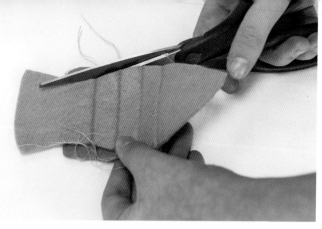

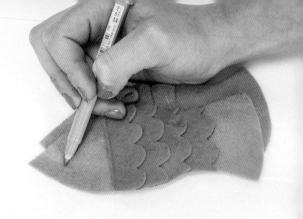

↑ **6** Trim any overhanging scales, using the edges of the fish body as your guide.

↑ **7** Repeat Steps 1–6 (page 213 and above) to add the other scales to the other fish body piece.

↑ **8** Decide where you want to place the eyes and mark with an erasable pen.

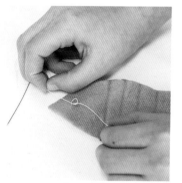

↑ **9** Sew a Vicki knot (page 29) to each fish body piece for the eye.

↑ **10** Place the fish body pieces wrong sides together and pin in place.

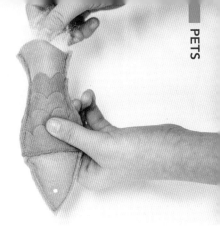

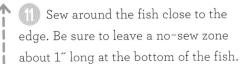

↑ ⑪ Sew around the fish close to the edge. Be sure to leave a no-sew zone about 1″ long at the bottom of the fish.

⋆TIP

Try to sew from the top to the bottom in the direction of the fish scales. It will be way easier, and you will be less likely to get the scales all bunched up under the presser foot.

↑ ⑫ Stuff the fish with a little stuffing; then add a spoonful of dried catnip.

Add some more stuffing until the fish is filled.

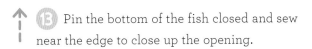

↑ ⑬ Pin the bottom of the fish closed and sew near the edge to close up the opening.

¡Finish Up!

Make as many fish as you like. Thread some embroidery floss through the top of each fish and tie them securely on the end of a wooden dowel.

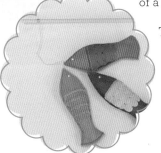

Tie on some yarn or maybe a feather or two, and your cat will be the luckiest kitty on the block!

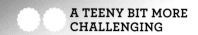
Super Dog Collar

No shopping at the pet store for you. You are going to learn to make your very own, totally custom pet collar!

› What Do I Need?

- ¾ yard of nylon webbing (1˝ wide)
- ⅛ yard of fabric
- Fun-colored sewing thread
- Adjustable plastic side-release or parachute buckle (1˝) (You can buy these at a craft store, or you can reuse these parts from an old collar!)
- Plastic slider buckle (1˝)
- 2 metal D-rings (1˝)
- Basic supplies (page 12)

› Special Skills

- Refer to The Rules of Sewing (page 9)
- Using an iron (page 21)

¡ Prepare the Pieces

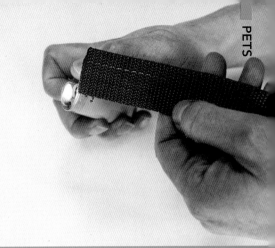

1 Cut the fabric to measure 3½″ × 28½″.

2 Ask an adult to gently burn both ends of the webbing using a butane lighter. This will prevent fraying.

- - - - - - - - - - - - - - - - - - →

¡ Let's Make It!

1 Fold in each end of the fabric strip ½″ and press with an iron

2 Fold the strip in half lengthwise with wrong sides together and press with an iron.

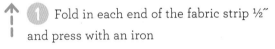

3 Open out the strip so you can see the crease and fold in each long edge to meet the center crease. Press with an iron.

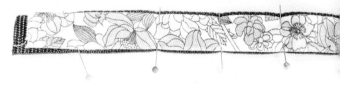

4 Refold the strip on the crease so the raw edges are on the inside and press really well with an iron.

5 Center the fabric piece on the nylon webbing and pin.

↑ ⑥ Stitch around the entire piece. Why not use a fun zigzag stitch?

↑ ⑦ Take an end of the webbing and attach half of the side-release buckle by threading the webbing above the plastic bar and then going back down through to the back. Make sure the buckle is facing up.

↑ ⑧ Pull the webbing out a couple of inches.

⑨ Use an erasable pen to mark a line 1˝ from the buckle. Sew on that line through both layers of webbing to attach the buckle.

↑ ⑩ Slide the D-rings onto the webbing up to the stitched line. Mark another line ½˝ from the D-rings and stitch on the line through both layers of webbing. This will hold the D-rings in place.

11 Slide the slider buckle on the other end of the webbing and move it down a few inches.

12 Now thread the other half of the side-release buckle onto the webbing in the same way as you did for the first half in Step 7 (previous page).

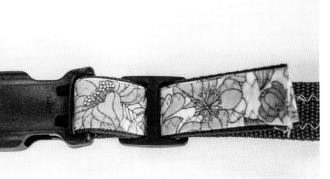

13 Pull a few inches of webbing through both the side-release buckle and the slider buckle. This helps make the collar adjustable.

Now all you have to do is choose which pet gets to wear this super-sweet collar. Here's a thought: why not make matching collars for all your four-legged friends?

Cozy Pet Bed

All pets need a cozy place to sleep. Here is your chance to make your kitty, your pooch, or even your bunny a bed worthy of wagging-tail royalty!

Finished size:
Approximately 26˝ × 26˝

❯ What Do I Need?

- 1⅝ yards of heavy decorator-weight fabric

- 26˝ × 26˝ pillow form

- 1 ball of yarn for pom-poms

- Pinking shears (*optional*—refer to the tip, page 222)

- Basic supplies (page 12)

❯ Special Skills

- Refer to The Rules of Sewing (page 9)

- Using an iron (page 21)

- Making a pom-pom (page 23)

- Sewing around a corner (page 19)

Prepare the Pieces

① Cut 1 piece of fabric to measure 26¾″ × 26¾″ for the front.

② Cut 2 pieces of fabric to measure 19″ × 26¾″ for the back.

☆TIP

Cut the pieces as shown. This is especially important if your fabric is narrower than 54″.

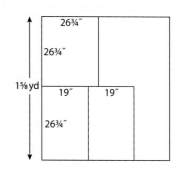

Let's Make It!

↑ *If you are using a ¼″ presser foot, don't forget to use washi tape as a guide to make the correct seam allowance width for this project (page 32).*

① Fold in a long end of each back piece ½″. Then fold in another ½″ and press with an iron.

↑ ② Pin the folds in place.

③ Sew nice and close to the folded edge on both back pieces.

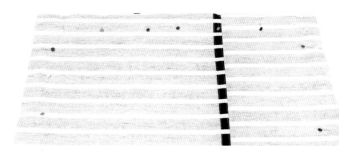

↑ ④ Lay the front pillow piece right side up on a flat surface.

⑤ Lay a pillow back piece right side facing down on the main piece. Line up the raw edges on 3 sides and pin in place.

↑ ⑥ Lay the other back piece on top. Line up the raw edges on 3 sides. The folded edge will overlap the folded edge of the other backing piece, but that's okay. Pin around all 4 sides of the pillow.

★ TIP

If you don't have pinking shears, you can set your sewing machine to a zigzag stitch and zigzag close to the edge around the entire pillow.

7 Sew around all 4 sides of the pillow with the edge of the presser foot on the edge of the fabric.

8 Use pinking shears to cut around all the raw fabric edges. This will stop them from fraying. Just don't cut the stitches!

9 Trim the corners, being careful not to cut into the stitching.

10 Turn your pet pillow right side out and give it a good press with an iron.

Finish Up!

We sewed some fun pom-poms to the corners of our pet beds just to add that something special!

1 Make 4 pom-poms.

2 Thread a needle with button thread and push it through the corner of the pillow. Tie a knot.

3 Push the needle through the center of the pom-pom and then back through the corner of the pillow. Repeat this a couple more times until the pom-pom is secure.

4 Tie a double knot with the thread ends.

5 Repeat Steps 2-4 with the other 3 corners.

6 Put the pillow form inside the cover and prepare for your pet to sleep tight!

Embroidered Pet Portraits

Immortalize your favorite pooch, bunny, kitty, or even lizard with these beyond-cute pet portraits. Make one for the pet lover in your life (and one for yourself!).

> What Do I Need?

- Inkjet printer fabric sheets (most measure 8½″ × 11″ and can be found in packages online or at a fabric store)

- Inkjet printer

- 8″ wood embroidery hoop

- Embroidery floss or perle cotton (size 8)

- Small beads (*optional*) (Make sure your needle can pass through the hole in the beads. If it is too tight, you may need a larger bead!)

- Basic supplies (page 12)

> Special Skills

- Refer to The Rules of Sewing (page 9)

- Using an iron (page 21)

- Hand sewing (page 26)

¡ Let's Make It!

THE IMAGE

1 Choose a digital photo of your favorite pet. You will be printing the image onto fabric, so it is important to make sure that everything is prepared correctly before you start the printing. Ask an adult if you need help.

2 Pull up the photo on the computer. Change the photo to black and white using the editing feature. It prints really well this way. Resize the photo so that the image of your pet will fit into an 8″ embroidery hoop.

3 Remove all the regular paper from your inkjet printer and load the inkjet fabric sheet into the paper tray. Following the manufacturer's instructions, print your photo onto the fabric.

4 Lay your printed image flat to dry for the time stated in the fabric sheet instructions, usually about 30 minutes.

5 Once the image is dry, use an iron with the steam turned off to iron over the image to set the ink.

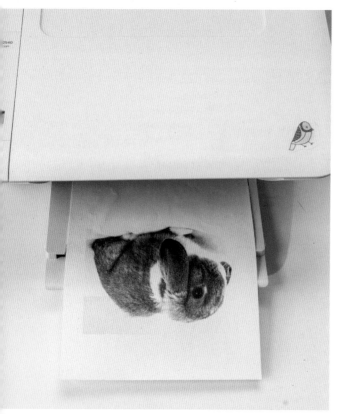

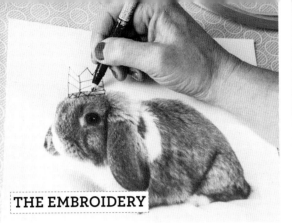

THE EMBROIDERY

1 Use an erasable pen to mark your embroidery design on the fabric. Try not to press too hard, because you do not want to damage the print. Be creative but don't make the design too complicated. Make each part of your design simple; you can add beads later!

2 Peel the paper from the back of the photo fabric.

Hoop the fabric. Don't worry if it's not perfectly centered—you can go back and rehoop it later.

How to Use an Embroidery Hoop

1 Loosen the little screw on top of the wood embroidery hoop. Separate the 2 hoops.

2 Place the inner hoop on a flat surface and lay the printed fabric on top with the image in the position you like.

3 Lay the loosened outer ring on top of the inner ring and push it down so that it firmly attaches on the outside.

4 Tighten the screw so that the fabric is held firmly in place.

Stitch on the Pet Photo

Use the stitch of your choice to embroider the design.

• Running stitch (page 26)

• Backstitch (page 28)

• Vicki knot (page 29)

For this project, we will be using a large backstitch.

1 Start by tying a knot at the end of an arm's length of floss.

2 Bring the needle through from behind the fabric and then push it back down through the fabric at the next point.

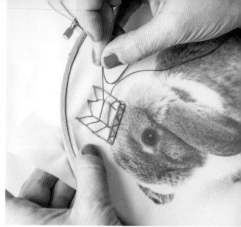

↑ ③ Bring the needle up again at the next point.

↑ ④ Now go backward and push it back down at the last point to fill in the line.

↑ ⑤ Continue stitching this way until the entire crown is filled.

ADDING BEADS

↑ ⑥ Carefully iron the crown to remove the erasable pen.

This is your project. Experiment with embroidery—I'm sure it will look great!

↑ ① Thread your needle with embroidery floss or perle cotton.

② Tie a knot in the end.

③ Bring the needle through the fabric from behind.

↑ ④ Thread a small bead in the needle.

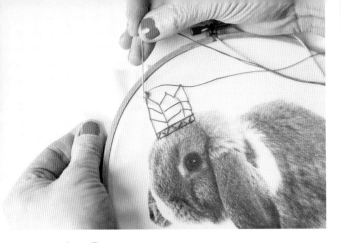
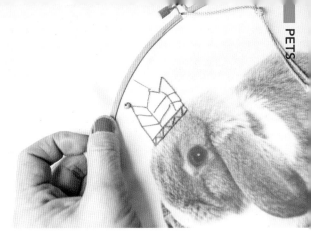

↑ **5** Take the needle back down to the back of the fabric and bring the needle back up at the next position.

↑ **6** Continue doing this until you have finished your design.

7 Tie a knot close to the back of the fabric when you get to the end.

¡Finish Up!

If you want to center the photo better, loosen the hoop screw, adjust the fabric, and retighten the screw. Trim around the fabric on the back of the hoop.

Hang your glorious portrait!

Embroidered Pet Portraits **227**

Patterns

DIY Fabric Design
Freezer-Paper Stencil

Blooming
Headband Circle
Cut 1.

MP3 Case Tab
Cut 1.

MP3 Case Heart
Cut 1.

Blossoming Necklace
and Flower Power Tee

Blooming
Headband Leaf
Cut 2.

Handy Pouch
Mushroom Dot
Cut 1.

Handy Pouch
Mushroom Dot
Cut 1.

Handy Pouch
Mushroom Dot
Cut 1.

Handy Pouch
Apple Stem
Cut 1.

Handy Pouch
Mushroom Cap
Cut 1.

Handy Pouch Apple Leaf
Cut 1.

Paper Flower Gift Toppers
Flower center

Cut 1 from crepe paper.

Handy Pouch
Mushroom Stem
Cut 1.

Handy Pouch Apple
Cut 1.

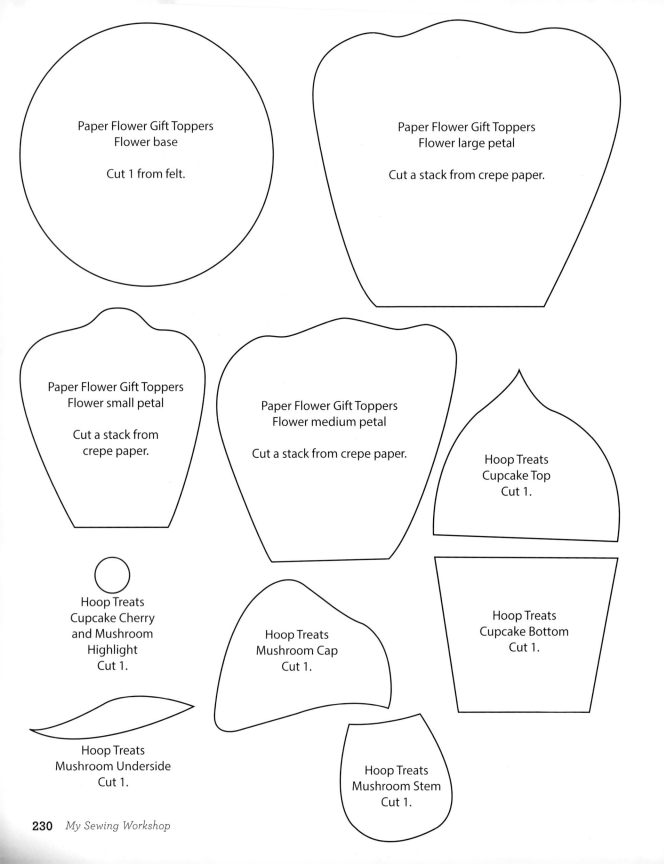

Paper Flower Gift Toppers
Flower base

Cut 1 from felt.

Paper Flower Gift Toppers
Flower large petal

Cut a stack from crepe paper.

Paper Flower Gift Toppers
Flower small petal

Cut a stack from
crepe paper.

Paper Flower Gift Toppers
Flower medium petal

Cut a stack from crepe paper.

Hoop Treats
Cupcake Top
Cut 1.

Hoop Treats
Cupcake Cherry
and Mushroom
Highlight
Cut 1.

Hoop Treats
Mushroom Cap
Cut 1.

Hoop Treats
Cupcake Bottom
Cut 1.

Hoop Treats
Mushroom Underside
Cut 1.

Hoop Treats
Mushroom Stem
Cut 1.

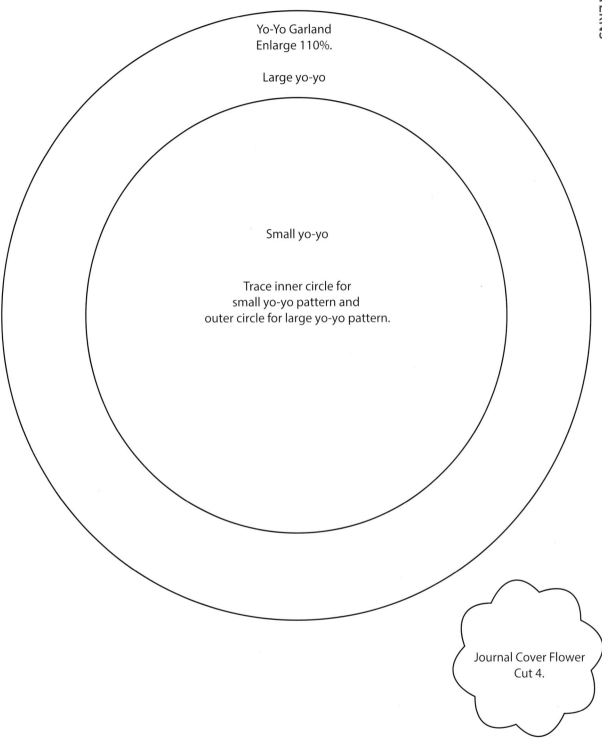

Yo-Yo Garland
Enlarge 110%.

Large yo-yo

Small yo-yo

Trace inner circle for
small yo-yo pattern and
outer circle for large yo-yo pattern.

Journal Cover Flower
Cut 4.

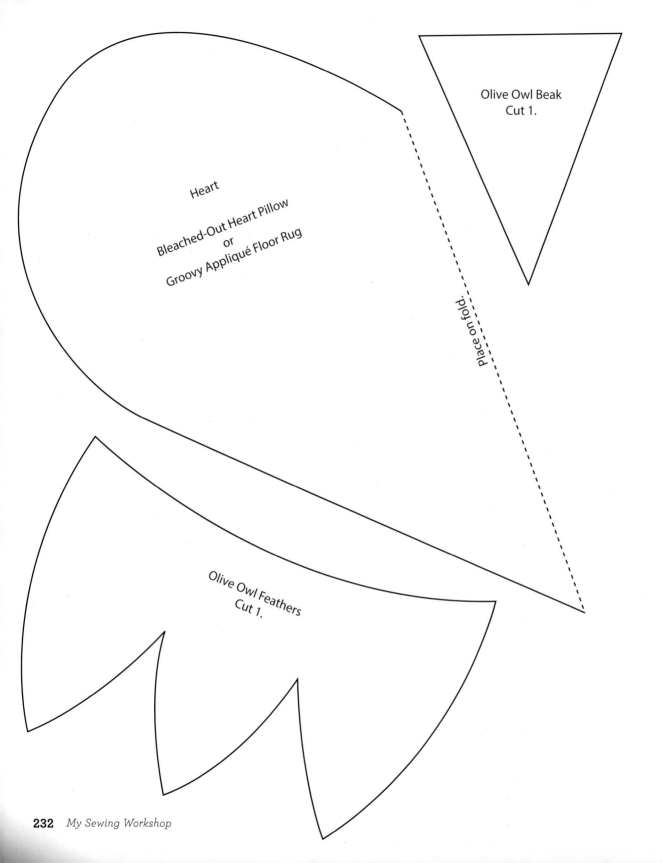

Olive Owl Beak
Cut 1.

Heart

Bleached-Out Heart Pillow
or
Groovy Appliqué Floor Rug

Place on fold.

Olive Owl Feathers
Cut 1.

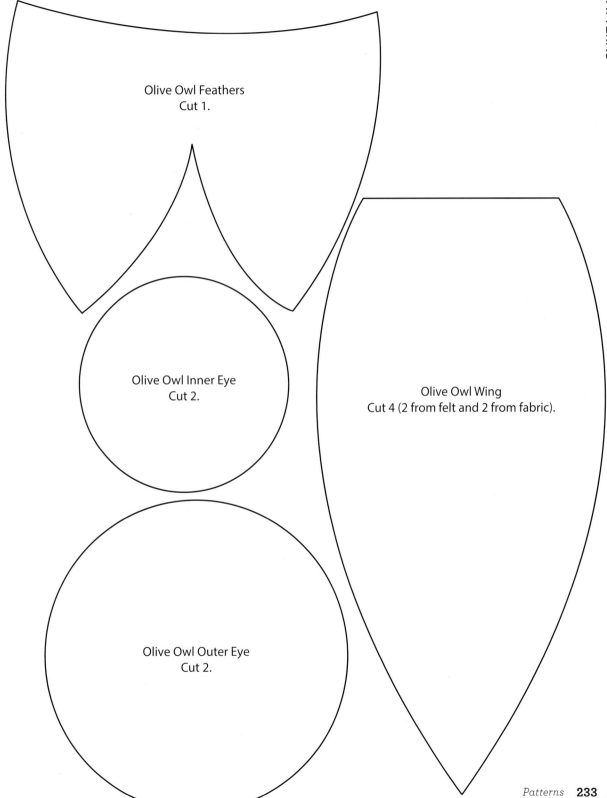

Olive Owl Feathers
Cut 1.

Olive Owl Inner Eye
Cut 2.

Olive Owl Wing
Cut 4 (2 from felt and 2 from fabric).

Olive Owl Outer Eye
Cut 2.

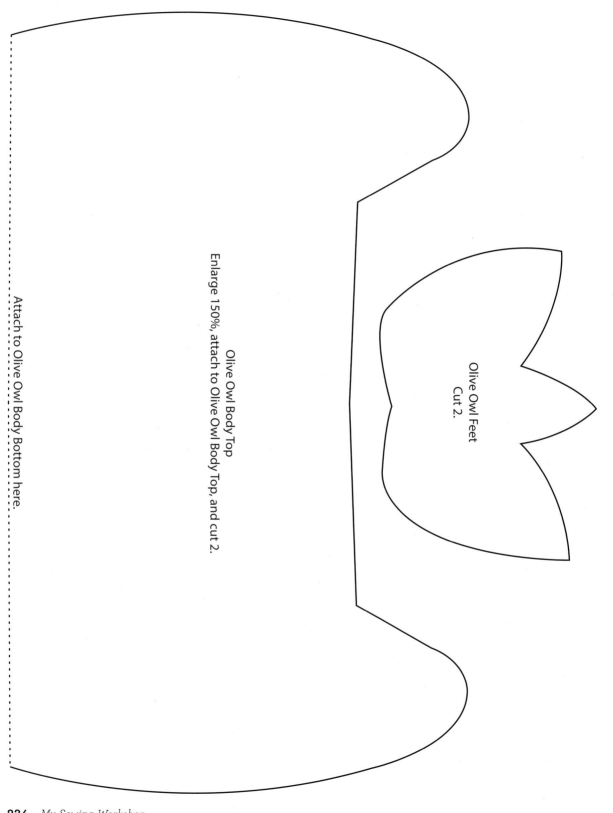

Attach to Olive Owl Body Bottom here.

Olive Owl Body Top
Enlarge 150%, attach to Olive Owl Body Top, and cut 2.

Olive Owl Feet
Cut 2.

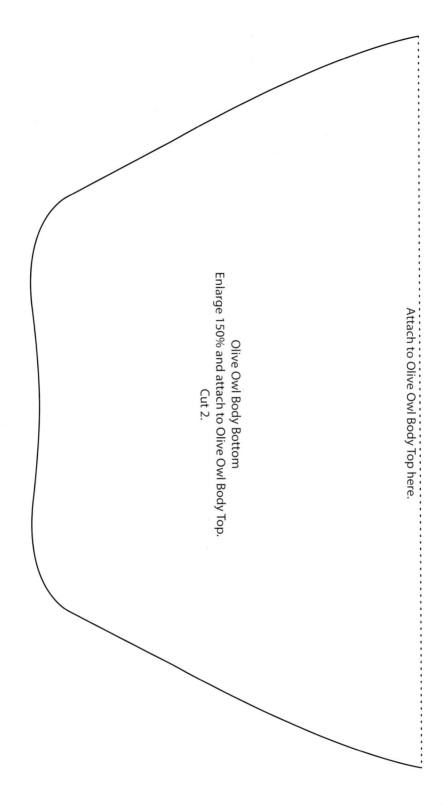

Attach to Olive Owl Body Top here.

Olive Owl Body Bottom
Enlarge 150% and attach to Olive Owl Body Top.
Cut 2.

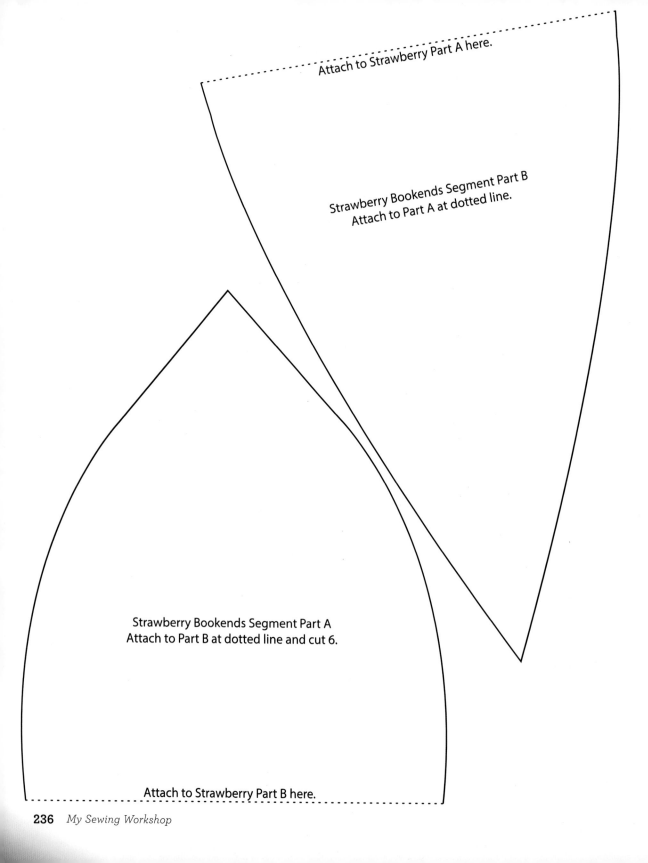

Attach to Strawberry Part A here.

Strawberry Bookends Segment Part B
Attach to Part A at dotted line.

Strawberry Bookends Segment Part A
Attach to Part B at dotted line and cut 6.

Attach to Strawberry Part B here.

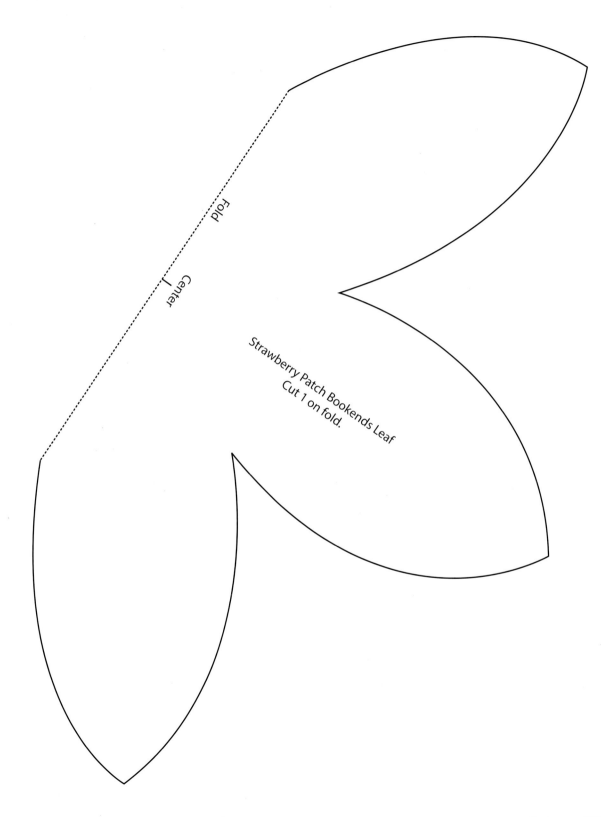

Fold

Center

Strawberry Patch Bookends Leaf
Cut 1 on fold.

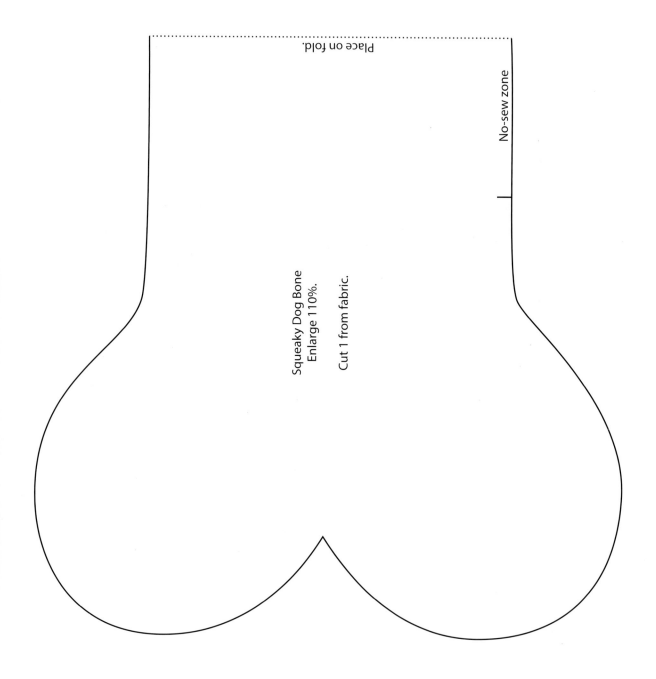

Place on fold.

No-sew zone

Squeaky Dog Bone
Enlarge 110%.

Cut 1 from fabric.

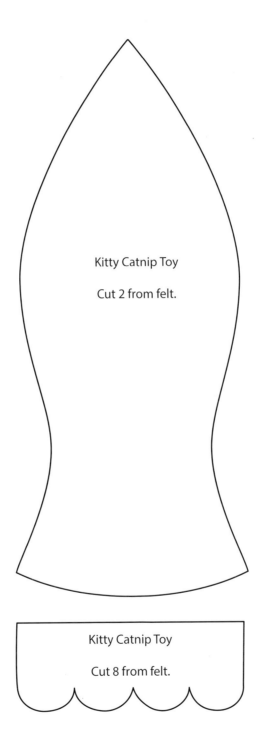

Kitty Catnip Toy

Cut 2 from felt.

Kitty Catnip Toy

Cut 8 from felt.

About the Author

ANNABEL WRIGLEY is an Aussie mom, author, designer, and owner of Little Pincushion Studio in Richmond, Virginia. She owns a creative studio where she teaches children to sew and helps them feel empowered on their creative paths. Her love of color and simple but creative designs are an important part of her everyday work. For the past decade of teaching, she has been guided by her philosophy of encouraging creativity and making it accessible to all children.

Follow Annabel online and follow on social media!

Website: annabelwrigley.com

Facebook: Little Pincushion Studio

Instagram: @littlepincushionstudio

Also by Annabel Wrigley: